COMPREHENSIVE FUNDRAISING CAMPAIGNS

A GUIDE FOR PRESIDENTS AND BOARDS

———————————

JAMES M. LANGLEY

———————————

ACADEMIC IMPRESSIONS | 2016
DENVER, CO

Published by Academic Impressions.

CR Mrig Company. 4601 DTC Blvd., Suite 800, Denver, CO 80237.

For reproduction, distribution, or copy permissions, or to order additional copies, please contact the Academic Impressions office at 720.488.6800 or visit:

http://bit.ly/2qbHuLr

Academic Impressions

ISBN: 978-1-948658-06-5

Printed in the United States of America.

OTHER BOOKS YOU MAY ENJOY

Comprehensive Fundraising Campaigns is one of a set of of four groundbreaking fundraising guides for university leaders written by James Langley. The others are:

- *Fundraising for Presidents*
- *Fundraising for Deans*
- *Fundraising for Boards*

Securing your institution's financial future isn't just about raising more dollars — it's about creating the conditions that foster continued and increased support. These four books rethink how your president, board members, academic deans, and other key stakeholders support the work of fundraising and donor relationship building. Learn practical strategies for involving those stakeholders at every stage of the donor lifecycle.

"This is is a treasure trove of great advice, forward-thinking reflections, and the tough, but much needed questions that presidents, boards, vice presidents and deans need to ask one another before embarking on a fundraising campaign." - *Matthew T. Lambert, Vice President for University Advancement, William & Mary*

Get all of James Langley's fundraising guides at:

https://www.academicimpressions.com/product/jim-langleys-fundraising-guides-university-leaders/

JAMES M. LANGLEY

CONTENTS

168 CHAPTER IX:
THE PRACTICALITIES OF CAMPAIGN PLANNING

179 CHAPTER X:
CONCLUDING THOUGHTS

183 ABOUT THE AUTHOR

JAMES M. LANGLEY

PREFACE

In the course of running three university campaigns, and in guiding dozens more as a consultant, I have seen virtually every college or university fall short of its full fundraising potential because of one significant, persistent, and largely unrecognized barrier: competing assumptions held by various institutional leaders about the keys to success and, therefore, the strategies and tactics that are most likely to produce it. Imagine, for instance, if a board chair believes that the key to success is a charismatic president; the president believes it is hiring a charismatic vice president for advancement, and the vice president for advancement believes it is a matter of hiring aggressive, extroverted fundraisers and holding them to meeting precise metrical goals. In those competing expectations, we see the weight of responsibility being shifted to another party, rather than the requisite acceptance of shared responsibility. We also see each party cleaving to a very incomplete part of a more complex reality.

In an earlier book, *Fundraising for Presidents: A Guide*, I stressed the importance of "the triangle of fundraising leadership," composed of the president, the board chair, and the vice president for advancement, and enumerated their shared responsibilities. "If this triangle of fundraising leadership is formed," I wrote, "and each party meets the expectations of the others, the institution will greatly improve its probability of philanthropic success."

If, however, each of these parties holds to a different theory of fundraising success, agreeing to a division of labor will prove difficult. Even if some nominal cohesion is achieved at the outset, it will come under strain as difficulties and frustrations are encountered in the course of a campaign.

Or imagine the leadership team of a political campaign composed of individuals with very divergent notions of the key to securing a majority of votes, and each second-guessing the other right up to Election Day.

In a higher education setting, it is not the least bit unusual to find competing assumptions about fundraising success, not only among members of the leadership triangle, but also among individual members of the board, members of the senior administration, and the senior staff of advancement. While a certain amount of this in a large, complex organization is inevitable and never fully resolvable, every effort to minimize it should be made when an institution resolves to conduct a comprehensive campaign.

> *A comprehensive campaign, by definition, is the means by which an institution seeks to advance its strategic priorities, an effort that requires focus, the marshaling of its human and financial resources, and the subordination of individual agendas to a common good.*

Institutions of higher learning must rise to the great strategic challenges of the day and develop campaign priorities that are responsive to current and emerging societal needs. Cohesion of purpose and clarity of mission is more important than ever before. This book, therefore, does not aspire to be a "how-to" manual. It seeks to ground board members, presidents, vice presidents for advancement, deans and other critical stakeholders with an objective and comprehensive understanding of what it takes to achieve higher levels of success in a campaign, and to sustain that growth well after the campaign is complete. In particular, it will review and elucidate under what conditions a comprehensive campaign should be considered, how it should be configured to align institutional competencies with societal needs and opportunities, how it can build and not deplete constituent strength, and why it must be conducted with the highest integrity.

Finally, it will call out, as no book before has done, the most constructive roles that boards (both governing boards and foundation boards) and individual board members can play in achieving these purposes, which are far greater and more strategic than the usual injunctions about "giving and getting." Indeed, greater optimization of a board's strategic oversight and individual board members' skills and experiences will be essential if institutions are to raise their game in these ever more challenging times.

A ROADMAP FOR THIS BOOK

Part 1: The Principles of Campaign Success

Introduction

Chapter I: So Much More Than Money

Institutional planners are encouraged to avoid the trap of striving to reach dollar goals for their own sake and to focus far more of their efforts on defining where the receipt of private funds will produce a significant and lasting impact, not only on the quality of the institution, but in the lives of those it serves.

Chapter II: The Case of the Disappointing Results

A fictional case study demonstrates why disappointing fundraising results are rooted in weak strategic planning and false assumptions, not in the tactical performance of one or more persons in campaign leadership positions.

Chapter III: President, Vice President of Advancement, and Board: The Most Productive Division of Labor

If a campaign is to reach its true potential, three key offices and the people leading them must have a unified grasp of the critical challenges ahead and the role that each must play in meeting them.

Chapter IV: Imagining and Implementing Better Ways

How to fully assess, in advance of a comprehensive campaign, an institution's fundraising potential by knowing how to measure the strength of the donor pipeline, the depth of constituent affiliation, the institution's ability to demonstrate greater agency through selected philanthropic investments, and institutional momentum.

Chapter V: Adapting to New Realities

A detailed review of specific strategies and approaches that will allow institutional leaders to adjust to changing economic, demographic and sociological shifts and to conduct campaigns that are more consonant with new and emerging philanthropic realities.

Chapter VI: Making Effective Use of Campaign Counsel

How to determine if your institution needs campaign counsel, and if so, what qualities, of the lead consult and the firm he or she represents, are most likely to complement your institution's strengths as well as compensate for any significant weaknesses.

Sidebar: The Real Utility of a Case for Support

This section (pages 116-118) enumerates the building blocks of an effective case for support as well as the optimal process for assembling the initial draft, vetting it with key constituents, and using it as an interactive field guide.

Part II: Organization and Execution

Chapter VII: From Planning to Implementation: The Role of the Board

A checklist of what institutional leaders should be thinking, planning and doing as a campaign moves toward and into the first phase of tactical implementation.

Chapter VIII: The Comprehensive Campaign in Phases

Describes the "emerging campaign" in seven key phases and contrasts this model with the more rigid "traditional campaign."

Chapter IX: The Practicalities of Campaign Planning

The considerations that should go into projecting a campaign total, how to go about budgeting for a campaign, the means of identifying the best volunteers and the best way to leverage their talents, and why stewardship should be seen as one of an institution's highest strategic priorities.

Chapter X: Concluding Thoughts

PART 1:
THE PRINCIPLES OF
CAMPAIGN SUCCESS

What should a comprehensive campaign look like if it is to navigate these new realities, and under what circumstances is it appropriate or inappropriate to launch one?

JAMES M. LANGLEY

INTRODUCTION

Before World War II, college and university fundraising campaigns, as we know them today, were relatively rare. They were more modest in their aspirations, briefer in their duration, and most likely to be conducted only by elite private colleges.

Following that war, first veterans armed with their GI Bill payments and then the large number of children that generation produced, increased the demand for a college education. More campaigns were conducted and more emphasis was placed on capital improvements for the construction of new buildings and/or the renovation of old ones. These efforts became known as "capital campaigns." Private colleges turned to their alumni and other donors to meet these needs while public institutions relied on state support to achieve these purposes.

Then, in accordance with the first immutable law of nature, everything became more complex. Major public institutions, realizing they had a chance to shape their destinies and mitigate the vicissitudes of public funding, entered the campaign arena. As they engaged their alumni about the institution's greater potential, they realized that campaigns could be employed to encourage support for a variety of purposes and to attract support from a variety of sources including independent philanthropists, foundations, and corporations. As donors were given more choices, philanthropic dollars began to flow toward people (students and faculty) and programs, and away from capital improvements. The term capital campaign, therefore, increasingly became a misnomer. The search for a more appropriate term found what seemed to be a more accurate rubric: the "comprehensive" campaign. All was right with the world, but only for a short while.

Comprehensive—a term employed to convey a set of strategic objectives by which an institution's mission could be advanced—came to be interpreted in a variety of ways, including counting everything from every source as part of the campaign, whether or not the gift was given in support of campaign objectives. Internal stakeholders began to assume the campaign must mean "something for everyone" or "everything we can think of."

As campaigns became more common, pursued ever-larger totals, and routinely met with success, it became all too easy for many board members and university officials to believe there was an endless amount of private support available for the asking. In the heady days of a strong economy and record levels of giving each year, rigorous strategic planning fell out of fashion. It was replaced by long lists of what could be done with more money, usually in the name of academic excellence, which would take the institution to the "next level."

> ### *In the heady days of a strong economy and record levels of giving each year, rigorous strategic planning fell out of fashion.*

This increasing drumbeat for more donations, backed only by broad rhetoric and imprecise promises, led to higher levels of donor fatigue and lower levels of alumni support. As the grip of the Great Recession was felt more acutely by larger swaths of society and as more alumni spent a large portion of their disposable income on repaying student loans, even the most loyal donors began asking hard questions and pushing back against broadly stated cases for support. At the same time, younger alumni began wondering if their alma maters were the most legitimate claimants for their philanthropy.

What, then, should a comprehensive campaign look like if it is to navigate these new realities, and under what circumstances is it appropriate or inappropriate to launch one?

College and university leaders must know what evidence to weigh before approving the additional expense of a campaign and, if one is warranted, how the institution can design and implement a campaign that optimizes its singular strategic potential given its history, core competencies, special circumstances, and unique assets. The material provided in this book will help those leaders ask the right questions; understand how to make the most effective contributions of time, talent, and treasure; and assess institutional fundraising effectiveness.

The generic campaign of the past few decades—in which institutions spent seven to 10 years in the field to secure funding for a wish list of projects, often celebrating the dollars raised more than the institutional purposes achieved or the societal services rendered—appears increasingly inefficient and ill-designed to navigate ever-more challenging realities, including lessening interest among potential donors. Yet the pursuit of private support, above and beyond the results it yields, keeps an institution in touch with its constituents, causes its leaders to listen, challenges their thinking, and helps them adjust to changing realities.

Let us explore, therefore, the design of a better campaign vehicle. The times demand it. Higher learning is critical to the expansion of opportunity, which has everything to do with a higher functioning economy, a more cosmopolitan culture, and a more vibrant democracy. The missions of our colleges and universities need to be advanced in more relevant and sustainable ways. The comprehensive campaign is a means of doing so, but the vehicle cannot be built on the assumptions of the past; it must be designed to navigate new realities and to demonstrate how it will make the institution most responsive to greater societal needs.

CHAPTER I:
SO MUCH MORE THAN MONEY

We are fortunate to live in a philanthropic culture in which a significant portion of our citizenry feels obliged to give of their time, talent, and treasure to improve the human condition. The truly philanthropic give a percentage of their earnings or wealth, no matter what. If they benefit from an expanding economy or good financial fortune, they give more. If they suffer from a contracting economy or a loss of wealth, they give less. Yet, remarkably, they continue to give. Donors, upon considering the fine work done by our institutions of higher learning, have risen to their calls many times. In fact, one hardly ever hears about a campaign that did not reach its goal in the requisite time.

> *The truly philanthropic give a percentage of their earnings or wealth, no matter what. Loyal, grateful alumni have been, far and away, higher education's greatest source of financial support.*

Higher education has achieved wider margins of excellence thanks to the awe-inspiring generosity of so many alumni, parents, friends, foundations, and corporations. In turn, higher education has converted that investment into greater societal gain by widening the circle of opportunity, fueling upward mobility, enriching culture, advancing science and technology, remediating suffering, inspiring innovation, and enriching the human condition in so many ways.

Yet as more institutions have launched more campaigns, success has become an increasingly relative term. Not every institution that announced it has raised $100 million, for instance, achieved that result in the same number of years as others did or financed the campaign at a similar level or converted dollars raised to similar institutional or societal gains. In a sampling of 10 institutions, public and private, that claimed to have raised that amount or more in the past decade, we see very different phenomena at work.

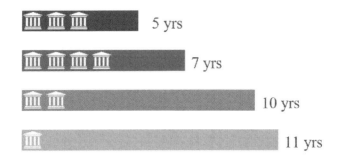

Taking a closer look:

- Three institutions reached that mark in five years of campaigning, four in seven years, two in 10 years, and one in 11 years.

- Two institutions raised 70 percent to 75 percent of that total for the stated purposes of the campaign, while three raised 60 percent to 70 percent for the original targets. Two others raised 50 percent to 60 percent of their totals for the original goals, while two others fell in the 40 percent to 50 percent range, and one raised less than 40 percent of its total for the designated purposes.

- Two institutions raised the requisite amount for designated capital improvements; three fell short by 20 percent or less; two by 30 percent or less; one by 40 percent or less; one by 50 percent or less; and one didn't even get close.

- Four institutions raised sufficient funds for new centers or institutes to allow those entities to be self-sufficient for a decade or more. Two incurred institutional obligations by accepting endowment gifts of $5 million that provided only 80 percent of the annual operating costs of the desired centers or institutes. Two had endowments whose earnings covered 50 percent of the annual costs, and two obligated the institution to match the $250,000 in earnings from those endowments each year from their precious unrestricted funds to keep the centers afloat.

- Three reached their $100 million total by counting only irrevocable deferred gifts from donors who were 70 years of age or older; three also included revocable deferred gifts from donors in the same age group; two included both revocable and irrevocable gifts at face value for all donors over 60; and two counted everything, including insurance policies at full face value for everyone regardless of age.

- Two reached that total by spending 10 percent or less on fundraising overhead; two spent 20 percent or less; four spent 30 percent or less; and two spent 40 percent or less (and all of them understated and/or underestimated their real costs).

- One institution's alumni participation rate increased by more than 1 percent over the life of the campaign; two saw their alumni participation rate decrease by an average of less than 1 percent; four institutions' decreased by less than an average of 2 percent; and three institutions' decreased by 3 percent or more (all but one of which reported "dollars up, donors down" each year).

All of these institutions declared victory for having achieved the same lofty goal of $100 million. Yet the celebration masked subtle but disturbing trends that have persisted in their respective cultures and across the land-scape of higher education over the previous two decades. These included the following:

- **Dollars up, donors down**: campaign successes became increasingly dependent on large gifts and mega-gifts given by relatively few donors;

- An almost 50-percent decline in the **volume of total alumni giving** annually (according to a Johnson, Grossnickle, and Associates study of data from the "Voluntary Support of Education" report); and

- The **loss of philanthropic support from "Millennials"**: only one- third of the members of this generation believe that their alma maters are deserving of their philanthropic support, according to a 2014 *Chronicle of Philanthropy* study.

These are not minor nor temporary vexations; they are trends of enormous strategic concern. "Dollars up, donors down" should not be ignored because it signifies the steady loss of higher education's most reliable and generous support, the impact of which will be felt for decades to come. The initial good news—dollars up—has a way of washing away the bad news that follows, but college and university leaders must reflect on and address the underlying issues with authenticity and urgency.

To put this issue in a different context and therefore see it in a more revealing light, imagine belonging to a church, club, or civic organization for 20 years and watching attendance at weekly services or meetings decline steadily. Imagine further how you would react if the leader of that organization announced his or her intention to raise more money than ever before, notwithstanding those declines in attendance. Your first and very natural reaction would be, "From whom?" If the leader persisted, painting a rosy picture based on an elaborate fundraising analysis, you might try to understand how it could be done. Your reasoning might go something like this:

The people most likely to support this organization are its members. If there are fewer of them, they will have to give more than ever before to get to the higher totals. They will have to give larger amounts more often. The more we lose members, the more pressure there will be on fewer people. At some point, there may be so few who have given so much and so often that they might just say, "Enough."

It would be hard to argue with your logic or your math. In the college setting, loyal alumni givers have been the most productive and consistent source of significant and transformational major gifts and estate gifts. While the full impact of the 50-percent drop in annual alumni giving cited above will not be felt all at once, it will be felt with increasing impact over time. Unlike the church, club, or civic organization, we cannot see the depletion of members, but it is no less real. We need to see, understand, and come to terms with factors and forces that may enhance or curtail an institution's supply lines.

Strategies employed by some campaigns have exacerbated these trends. No truly responsible fiduciary should endorse a campaign that, at best, ignores the new strategic realities or, at worst, contributes to their acceleration. Contentment with "dollars up, donors down" must be replaced by the search for more sustainable models that produce more broad-based philanthropic cultures. If not, the trend for most will be "dollars and donors down." And that pattern, by mathematical certainty, can only continue for so long.

> *Contentment with "dollars up, donors down" must be replaced by the search for more sustainable models that produce more broad-based philanthropic cultures.*

As campaigns meet or exceed their dollar goals, who asks if the money was raised in the most expeditious and cost-effective manner, placed the institution on stronger strategic foundations, served to broaden or deepen constituent relations, or rendered a significant return to the community or society? Many presidents and fundraisers move on to more lucrative positions after a campaign, and consultants celebrate client victories to secure more clients, but who takes stock of what actually happened to the institution? What successes can continue to be leveraged for greater institutional momentum? What deficiencies were revealed, and how can they be mitigated? Which of them are most consequential and need to be addressed quickly?

Who bears the responsibility for asking the right questions before, during, and after a comprehensive campaign? The answer is clear: those with the greatest fiduciary responsibility, the board members. A fiduciary, after all, is one charged with the safekeeping and management of a trust or asset, so a full strategic assessment of the state of that asset must be conducted before and after a campaign. In assessing the workability or impact of a campaign, important questions include the following:

- Is the additional expense of the campaign warranted? That is, could the institution raise the same or more money without all the campaign hoopla? How much of the total will be raised for specific stated purposes? In what tangible ways will the institution and those it serves be made better? Will the money raised strengthen or extend the financial core of the institution?

- Will the institution see an upsurge in planned gifts, outright gifts, or endowment gifts as result of entering a campaign? If so, what aspects of the campaign will promote that upsurge?

- What will the year-over-year cash flow look like in five years, 10 years, and beyond 10 years? How much has come in the form of deferred gifts, and over what time-span are they expected to mature?

- How will the institution's reputation among key constituents be affected? What baseline studies have been done to help leaders understand changing levels of affinity and affiliation among possible donors?

- Can the institution avoid the larger national trend of "dollars up and donors down"? How will leaders monitor attrition of current and loyal donors, and what are the strategies for counter-acting it?

- Are accountability and stewardship built into planning to ensure that donors feel the institution delivered on the promises? How readily and tangibly did the institution convert new levels of investment into new levels of performance and achievement?

- Will the campaign help develop a stronger culture of philanthropy or a greater sense of entitlement among internal stakeholders? Will the advance-ment operation and the advancement culture be strengthened? Has the institution strengthened or weakened the ability to raise more money in the future?

These are the questions that institutional leaders must explore in depth to ensure their institutions design and execute campaigns that achieve fundamental and sustainable strength, rather than short-term victory.

Clearly, there is much more to campaigns than the dollar amount to be raised and the corollary tactical concerns. To navigate through these new realities and to achieve higher levels of sustainable institutional relevance, all the key players in a comprehensive campaign—the board, president, vice president for advancement, deans, and institutional thought leaders—need to be looking at the same set of facts. This is not always the case because some individuals may rely on myths or clichés such as the following to form their views of campaigns:

MYTHS ABOUT CAMPAIGNS

— "There's a lot of low-hanging fruit out there."

— "We have wealthy donors just waiting to be asked. We have to be more aggressive in asking."

— "We have all sorts of buildings around here with no names and lots of rich people out there who want their names on things."

— "All we need to do is hire more fundraisers. We need a better elevator speech."

— "We need a president who can sell ice to the Eskimos."

In the absence of facts, research, analysis, and good-old-fashioned listening, speculation abounds, competing theories emerge, and expectations skyrocket. If expectations are not met, no matter how unrealistic they were to begin with, blame begins to be apportioned, anxiety mounts, organizations lurch, and productivity falters.

Indeed, the case study in the following chapter, albeit fictionalized, continues to play out in varying degrees across higher education. It demonstrates a central tenet of this book:

THE CORE IDEA

Successful campaigns leverage existing assets; unsuccessful campaigns attempt to compensate for existing weaknesses. Therefore, the best way to prepare for a comprehensive campaign—well before

THE CORE IDEA, CONTINUED

asking others to give of their time, talent, and treasure—is for institutional leaders to determine and invest appropriate assets to minimize structural weaknesses, including weak academic programs, inefficient or bloated aspects of the administration or anything that leads to the non-academic attrition of students. They will then be prepared to turn to their donors to leverage strength, widen the margins of excellence, propel the organization from good to great or great to extraordinary, and yield tangible and lasting improvements to community and society.

KEY TAKEAWAYS

- Boards and presidents need to ensure that their institutions think about comprehensive campaigns in more wide-ranging ways than just how many dollars might be raised, including how the college or university might build a broader, more enduring community of shared purposes.

- Boards need to serve as an external reality check for the institution's internally generated aspirations to ensure they are sensible, strategic, and sustainable.

- Campaigns should be launched to leverage assets, not to compensate for institutional weaknesses.

CHAPTER II: THE CASE OF THE DISAPPOINTING RESULTS

A Case Study

The leaders of fictional Steadman University—including the board chair, president, and vice president for advancement—believed they had been duly diligent before approving "Ever Steadman," a seven- year comprehensive campaign designed to strengthen three pillars of institutional excellence: student support, faculty support, and capital improvements.

With the usual injunction that it would "take more money to raise more money," the board was advised by a fundraising consultant to approve an increase of 20 percent in the advancement office's base budget, plus a one-time increase representing 2 percent of the campaign's total goal for collateral material, marketing, and campaign events. The consultant reassured the board regarding the university's greater fundraising potential using an impressive array of analyses, including "wealth screening" that showed the number of prospects available at various levels of giving. When added up, these came to an eye-popping sum.

Many members of the board were happy to see that the projected fundraising capacity was far greater than had been secured previously because they themselves had been asserting that the potential was there for years. Now they actually had facts to corroborate those strong opinions. Other board members were happy to see so many new names with such significant means on the prospect list, while silently hoping that it meant there would be less pressure on them to give. Still other board members were wondering why seemingly obvious things had not been done before and how it was that a consultant could bring so much good news so quickly.

Meanwhile, in Steadman's advancement operation, a different reality was playing out. The frontline fundraisers were struggling to meet their annual performance goals, notwithstanding the fact that all but two of them were making a valiant effort. Each had been assigned a portfolio of prospects as part of their normal workload, prior to the beginning of the comprehensive campaign, whom they were assured had been culled from larger lists that had been put through wealth screening to ensure that they were the most promising. Yet when these fundraisers made calls and/or sent emails to these prospects, very few responded. Even the best of these fundraisers were only getting a response from one out of every 15 prospects contacted, and some of those responses were very tentative:

> *I'm not in a position to give anything, but I can meet you for coffee ... but I only have 30 minutes.*

Others were outright dismissive:

> *Sure, I'm happy to talk, but I'm going to make the same contribution I have for the past 14 years.*

While some of the fundraisers had developed the coping skill of pretending everything was going fine when it really wasn't, others began to offer theories to explain their inability to secure appointments with the prospects, including the following:

- The research office wasn't giving them very good prospects.

- The president and vice president had scooped up all the good prospects.

- The wealth screening that the vice president had paid too much for was worthless.

- The president didn't have vision.

- We don't spend enough on marketing.

- We don't spend enough on alumni relations.

- Our events aren't very good.

- Our bosses don't know what they're doing.

Yet in the face of gathering gloom, the more optimistic staff members were quick to point to the impending campaign, asserting it would be just the jolt old Steadman needed. "The campaign will get everyone excited," they said. "We'll have more events and really cool promotional literature. And when the president announces a big gift, everyone else will want to jump on board."

And so it was that Ever Steadman went forward boldly into what is known as the quiet phase of the campaign, a period in which the most promising of prospects were asked to sit for confidential interviews conducted by the campaign consultant. In these interviews, the consultant, armed with the newly minted case statement outlining reasons for support, asked these most promising prospects (many of whom were on the board) if the university was moving in the right direction, if they thought the campaign would accelerate the growth of the institution's stature, if they intended to "participate" in the campaign, and to what degree.

The board had already voted for the campaign and committed significant institutional resources to it, so the members interviewed in this "feasibility study" generally agreed that the university was indeed moving in the right direction and that the campaign could only help. When the consultant presented the interviewees with a gift pyramid and asked at which level they saw themselves giving, most pointed close to or at the top. Their reasons for doing so were many and complex, including the following:

- They thought they might like to give that much someday.

- They might consider giving that amount, if they were made the next board chair.

- They wanted the consultant to know they had the means to do so.

- They might be able to give that much in an estate gift.

- They might be able to give that much if this new company or that new stock really took off.

When the consultant reported to the advancement committee of the board that the feasibility study had revealed even more potential than had been anticipated, the board agreed to bump the campaign total from $160 million to a nice even $200 million. At the consultant's recommendation, the president and the board agreed to officially launch the campaign when the totals neared the halfway mark, which was projected to take two years. Planning for the grand public launch, however, should begin in earnest one year hence, advised the consultant.

The first year of active fundraising for Ever Steadman unfolded well but without a windfall. Those who gave most generously were those who had given most generously before or had given loyally over decades. The president felt a little skeptical about Marian McGillicuddy, whom he had pegged as a "piker." Although she had given for 23 consecutive years, she never gave more than $10,000 at a time. When asked by the vice president of advancement to meet with her one more time, the president retorted, "If I had a dollar for every time I visited her, I could give a lot more than she has or will." Yet a few days after that dreaded meeting, she left the president a voicemail saying she would give $1.8 million.

As a result, the president didn't challenge the vice president's requests for the next seven months, even as he met with the same folks he had been meeting with since he first took the job. Further, many of the individuals who had emerged as golden in the wealth screening process were not receptive to visits from anyone from the university, even the president. Those who did agree to meet with the president were polite, but less than forthcoming about their willingness to give. Those who were willing to discuss giving had very strong feelings about what they would support and showed little interest in Steadman's campaign literature or its menu of giving opportunities. After a series of such meetings, the president groused, "No one is interested in giving to us or meeting our needs; it's all about what they want to achieve."

Meanwhile, back at the advancement office, life hadn't gotten any easier. Prospects were still not receptive to fundraisers' requests, notwithstanding the Ever Steadman literature that had been sent in advance. Three fundraisers announced their decisions to leave, although none had been at Steadman for more than three years. The pessimists seized on their departures as support for one of the various "what's wrong" theories noted above, while the optimists predicted that a few mega-gifts were in the works and the public phase would create a raft of new opportunities.

At the end of the first year of the quiet phase of the campaign, Ever Steadman had secured $37,324,288 in gifts and pledges, not an insignificant sum, but substantially less than what many board members thought possible, especially if the $200-million campaign was predicated on securing approximately half that amount in the first two years. By that calculation, the campaign was well off track.

But something else was nagging at some board members, a kind of disappointment in the predictable, pedestrian way the campaign was unfolding. Notwithstanding the healthy increases in budgeting for campaign operations and collateral material, the campaign just seemed like more of the same: the same people giving (albeit more in several surprising cases); the same alumni attending events and expressing the same interests or views they always had; and the same lectures being delivered by institutional leaders to the board urging members to give more and be more helpful with fundraising. What happened to all those promising prospects revealed in wealth screening? Why weren't they giving more?

Whenever doubt and misgiving creep into a culture, blame is sure to follow. And so it was at Steadman. Wherever two or three board members gathered, theories were advanced as to why Ever Steadman had gotten off to such a "slow start." While some trustees were more circumspect and modulated in their concerns, it wasn't long before the president, vice president, campaign consultant, and board chair were the targets of varying degrees of criticism. The disappointing performance was ascribed to numerous factors, including the following:

- The board chair was too "chummy" with the president.

- The board chair was not visible enough in the community or, because he had retired from his business, had lost his influence.

- The president lacked a compelling vision; wasn't an inspiring orator; or wasn't decisive.

- The vice president wasn't aggressive enough; wasn't tough enough on her staff; or wasn't a good manager.

- The president and the vice president didn't work as a team.

- The president was frustrated with the vice president.

- The vice president was frustrated with the president.

- The right consultant had not been chosen; the consultant's advice was not being taken; the consultant's firm was too big; the consultant's firm was too small.

- There are people out there dying to be asked, and no one is asking them.

To solve this mystery, let us step away from Steadman so that we can better understand the factors and forces that lead to the building of robust philanthropic cultures and typically lead to successful campaigns.

Philanthropic Patterns

By studying philanthropic patterns unfolding over decades and across numerous institutions, we can see four powerful elements at work: appreciation, affiliation, agency and accountability.

Appreciation

Appreciation, according to the testimony of consistently generous alumni, is predicated on the broad belief that the value of their education greatly exceeded the price of tuition. It is also founded on an undying gratitude to a few professors (and sometimes coaches) who caused them to realize that they were capable of more than they had once thought. Such alumni speak most appreciatively of even demanding and exacting professors, sometimes ones who issued failing grades, because of the competencies they inculcated—and the difference those competencies made over time.

Surprisingly, those alumni who worked on campus when they were students are far more apt to express philanthropic appreciation than those who received high-end scholarships or "full rides." Indeed, according to a Langley Innovations analysis of 52 institutions, the recipients of particularly prestigious scholarships are far less likely to give back, even to the scholarship programs that once sponsored them. Other factors that deepened their appreciation, such generous alumni say, included rituals that moved them emotionally (primarily freshman convocation and commencement), traditions that spanned the generations, and the feeling of being a member of a distinct or distinguished community.

Indeed, according to a Langley Innovations analysis of 52 institutions, the recipients of particularly prestigious scholarships are far less likely to give back, even to the scholarship programs that once sponsored them.

Appreciation is also relative to one's perception of the cost/value proposition. If an alumnus or alumna is philanthropic by nature and believes that the value of his or her education over time has been significantly greater than what it cost, he or she is more likely to feel compelled to give back to make up for the clear disparity between cost and value. Alumni who graduated before 1975 are much more apt to feel that the value of their college education greatly exceeded the cost. But, with sustained double-digit increases in tuition becoming more prevalent throughout the 1980s and 1990s, graduates of those years, particularly those who incurred significant debts, came to see cost as equal to value provided. As a result, they have proved less receptive to the call from their alma maters to give back. Indeed, many felt they were giving back by writing the check every month to pay off their student loans, often for 10 or more years.

Affiliation

Affiliation, that is, remaining actively engaged with one's alma mater after graduation, when added to amount of appreciation felt, greatly increases the likelihood of an alumnus giving over the decades. Volunteers, according to a study done by the Fidelity Gift Fund and Volunteer Works, give 10 times the amount to their institution of choice than those who only make donations. Further, the sooner after graduation an alumnus becomes actively engaged, the more he or she is likely to remain engaged and to give more with every passing decade. Alumni who give $1 million or more to their alma maters in any given year have given, on average, for 14 previous years, according to a Langley Innovations study of more than 1000 gifts given to more than 100 institutions over the past 20 years. The ardor of even the most appreciative alums, on the other hand, is likely to dim with the passing of time and in the absence of affiliation.

And, as we have learned in an extensive study of thousands of alumni across dozens of private and public institutions, conducted by the Collaborative Innovation Network for Engagement and Giving, even appreciative alumni fall away when they begin to feel that their alma mater "does little to reach out to me beyond asking for money." What generous alumni want from their colleges and universities is similar to what students want: the ability to continue to learn from exceptional faculty members and talented peers. In the main, they are not interested in affiliating with their alumni association if it does not meet those desires.

What generous alumni want from their colleges and universities is similar to what students want: the ability to continue to learn from exceptional faculty members and talented peers.

Agency

Agency, one of the most overlooked elements of enduring philanthropic compacts, also motivates a sustaining donor. Agency is the belief that he or she is not just giving *to* his or her college or university, but also *through* it to create a better world. It rests on the idea that a better world can be broadly conceived, such as believing that one's alma mater serves the purposes of democracy by widening the circle of opportunity or by serving as an engine of upward mobility. Agency also can be more narrowly interpreted, as in the case of an accounting alumna who believes her alma mater is having a disproportionately positive impact on professional practice in that field.

The element of agency, generally in combination with appreciation and affiliation, explains why alumni give remarkably generous gifts to colleges and universities with the largest endowments. We often hear the incredulous outside observer of this phenomenon ask, "Why on earth would anyone give so much to a university that has billions of dollars in endowment? They don't need the money!"

The reality is that institutional need is not a driving factor in the most significant philanthropic commitments. If, for instance, you lost a loved one to a terrible disease and thus became passionately motivated to exercise your full philanthropic resources to help others so afflicted, you would not give to the medical center or research institution that most needed the money, but rather to the one that had the greatest potential to rid the world of that dread disease.

In fact, over-emphasizing basic needs—such as a college charging more than $35,000 in annual tuition while asserting it requires contributions to its annual fund "to keep the lights on"—undercuts an institution's larger philanthropic appeal. Agency is not about the margin of survival; it is about the margin of excellence—about demonstrating how philanthropic investment can take an institution or some critical part of it "from good to great."

Agency is not about the margin of survival; it is about the margin of excellence—about demonstrating how philanthropic investment can take an institution or some critical part of it "from good to great."

Accountability

Accountability, with every passing year grows in importance as the competition for private support, particularly the largest gifts, becomes more intense. Demonstrating institutional accountability is about so much more than thanking and recognition. Indeed, client research conducted by Langley Innovations in which surveys of constituents from approximately 30 institutions reveals that most major donors feel sufficiently thanked and recognized, but under-informed about the impact of their gift. A 2012 Burk Donor Survey of 15,000 donors in the U.S. and Canada showed that many donors were willing to give more if they better understood the impact of their giving.

Accountability, however, is not something that can be promised or put off until after a gift agreement has been reached, it must be projected in white papers and proposals, either because many donors will expect it or because it will be critical to the making of an effective proposal and to justifying the amount requested. Institutions that project ambitious, but attainable strategic goals and demonstrate how they will hold themselves accountable to their own aspirations, will gain more traction with the most discerning, but generous donors.

Clues and Lessons

With that knowledge in hand, let us return to Steadman to better understand the reasons for what was seen as Ever Steadman's "disappointing start." Telltale clues and lessons include the following:

Clue #1

> Steadman's campaign was "designed to strengthen three pillars of institutional excellence: student support, faculty support, and capital improvements."

Reasonable Deductions: This rationale for giving is dated, stale, and inward looking. It expects people to give to Steadman in the name of institutional excellence, but outlines no opportunity for them to create a better world through giving to the university. As such, it fails to take advantage of the power of agency. While support for students and faculty and for certain capital improvements may be integral to the university's ability to make a greater contribution to society, Steadman's case for support does not explain how or why that could happen. It offers only categories of giving and process; it does not speak to quantitative or qualitative outcomes that will be achieved if the requested funds are received. Only institutions that have developed a broad base of constituent support and have not conducted recent back-to-back campaigns can get away with a broad-based appeal such as this one.

Steadman, as we will see, did not pick up on evidence of an eroded or insufficiently developed base of support.

Clue #2

"The consultant reassured the board regarding the university's greater fundraising potential using an impressive array of analyses, including 'wealth screening,' that showed the number of prospects available at various levels of giving. When added up, these came to an eye-popping sum."

Reasonable Deductions: Two broad and false assumptions were made in the consultant's report, and these were compounded by the way the assumptions were interpreted by the board:

- Not all wealthy people are philanthropic, and many of the records accumulated in wealth screening, particularly relating to individuals holding large amounts of real estate, actually may be considered negative indicators of philanthropic intent. Many true philanthropists live below their means and are not given to conspicuous consumption and, therefore, are not easily discoverable through wealth screening.

- Even if many of the prospects unearthed in the wealth screening were philanthropic, they could not be converted easily to donors if they had not previously donated to Steadman. Remember that the average donor who gives $1 million or more to a college or university typically already has been giving to it for 15 years. And people who are truly philanthropic frequently become affiliated with causes. So, if Steadman had not engaged these alumni in recent years, or if it had let decades elapse before reconnecting with alumni who have become financially successful, it has years of work to do to reintroduce them to the university and prove to them that, of all the places they could give to, Steadman is the best place they can give to fulfill their values.

Clue #3

"Other board members were happy to see so many new names with such significant means on the prospect list, while silently hoping that it meant there would be less pressure on them to give."

Reasonable Deductions: If a board votes to approve a campaign, its members cannot treat it like an out-of-body experience. Board members of four-year institutions give, on average, 25 percent of all individual campaign and 20 percent of the campaign total at liberal arts schools, according to a 2015 Marts & Lundy study, and usually are the first to make campaign commitments. If those who know the institution best, who have the most access to information about it, and who interact most closely with the president do not support the institutional goals the campaign represents, it is naïve to expect those with less access to the institution to provide greater support. Board members who do not believe in the campaign purposes and are not prepared to support them should express their concerns when the vote is taken and reassess their board service.

Board members of four-year institutions give, on average, 25 percent of all individual campaign and 20 percent of the campaign total at liberal arts schools, and usually are the first to make campaign commitments.

Clue #4

"Even the best of these fundraisers were getting a response from only one out of every 15 prospects contacted."

Reasonable Deductions: This often over-looked metric reveals a lack of receptivity to giving to Steadman. We can assume that the advancement operation has done a reasonably good job of identifying those who have the strongest likelihood of giving to the university and that the frontline fundraisers are working with a set of qualified leads. Thus, when even the best fundraisers are meeting with this level of resistance or lack of interest, it reveals a loss or lack of depth in its pool of constituents. Research conducted by Cindy Cox Roman of WIT Consulting in Washington, D.C., reveals the major reasons that otherwise philanthropic graduates of even the most prominent institutions of higher learning are opting to give less to their alma maters.

The reasons include:

REASONS OTHERWISE PHILANTHROPIC ALUMNI GIVE LESS TO THEIR ALMA MATERS

- I feel that I've paid enough already in tuition;

- I don't think the school really needs the money;

- I haven't been given a good enough reason to give;

- I don't feel a deep emotional connection to the school;

- They haven't done enough to connect with me beyond asking for money;

- I feel like donations go into a "black hole";

- I want my donations to go for a specific purpose and I don't have that option;

- I feel like a small gift won't make a difference;

- I'm confused about the difference among various fundraising programs;

- I'm unhappy with the direction the school is taking;

- They haven't been aggressive enough in asking for the money; and

- There has been bad publicity about the school.

Steadman's inability to assess existing weaknesses in constituent engagement before initiating the campaign caused it to attempt to launch its campaign from a weak foundation. This weakness then becomes compounded by other factors.

Clue #5

"The campaign will get everyone excited," they said. "We'll have more events and really cool promotional literature."

Reasonable Deductions: A campaign is a way of leveraging what exists, not a way to compensate for what is missing. Steadman lacks constituent depth, and its case statement fails to cite specific differences that donations will make—a bad combination. Launching a campaign will not compensate for those weaknesses or draw forward large numbers of people who haven't given or been involved. That's why the same people showed up for the new campaign's events.

Using a metaphor from another sector, one must build the congregation before passing the collection basket to a depleted, under-inspired congregation. Board members might imagine themselves in this scenario:

SCENARIO

You answer a knock on your door one evening to find a pious and genial looking gentleman holding a basket, the kind that is passed at church during the offering. He extends the basket to you.

"Please give," he says to you.

"To what?" you ask.

"To the United Church."

"What?" you sputter. "I'm not a member there anymore."

"Yes, but didn't we do good things for you?" asks the genial gentleman.

"Well, yes, I suppose, but that was … more than 20 years ago."

"Wasn't our influence lasting? Aren't you forever grateful?"

"Well, I suppose, but I'm now involved with another church."

"Haven't you gotten our newsletter? We're doing some really good things."

"I'm sure you are," you say, "but lots of organizations are doing good things, including my church and several other charities with which I'm involved."

"Here, please read this brochure. We have several giving opportunities."

"Look," you say, "I haven't heard from you in 20 years. Why should I be eager to give?"

"Well, would you give if I sent you a tweet every now and then?"

"Please don't. I'm afraid there's some sort of terrible mistake here. I haven't been in your congregation in ages. I don't know your minister. I haven't heard him preach."

"Would you like to meet Minister Bob?"

"No," you say. "I'm sure he's a fine man, but I'm happy with my new church."

"We have lots of naming opportunities—the foyer or the rec room or the …"

"No, I have no interest in having my name plastered anywhere, much less some place that I never go and haven't been affiliated with."

"May I come again?"

"No, it would do no good." As you slowly close the door, you see a rather handsome four-color brochure sliding under it.

If a prospect hasn't been engaged or involved or hasn't been informed as to why he or she should care about the health of an institution, there is little the most earnest, determined, or genial fundraiser can do, and no collateral material, new media, or gimmick will help. Sometimes board members don't understand the slow, but more certain rhythms of true philanthropy, including the stubborn fact, as noted previously, that long-time givers are the most likely to make significant donations. Hiring more fundraisers to knock on even more doors or knock harder doesn't change the rhythms of philanthropy. Front-line fundraisers are the most expensive part of a fund-raising organization and should only be deployed to harvest appreciation and agency and/or to explore the potential for aligning interests with philanthropists whose passions correspond to institutional purposes.

Frontline fundraisers are the most expensive part of a fundraising organization and should only be deployed to harvest appreciation and agency and/or to explore the potential for aligning interests with philanthropists whose passions correspond to institutional purposes.

Marketing has its place, but it does not build community or relationships. You can't "market" prospects into philanthropic submission. Inundating a prospect with campaign material will not, through its sheer volume, eventually prompt a gift. Impersonal means of communication, including broad institutional promotional pieces, cannot compensate for the absence of building interpersonal relationships. Productive relationships cannot be built if both parties are not willing to listen and work at aligning purposes.

Clue #6

"When the consultant presented them with a gift pyramid and asked them at which level they saw themselves giving, most pointed close to or at the top."

Reasonable Deductions: The best predictor of what people will do in the future is not what they say in the present, but what they have done in the past. Steadman's consultant was naïve to assume that people would give at the level indicated during the feasibility study's interviews. It would have been wiser to compare the indicated level to the level of previous giving to Steadman or anywhere else to extrapolate a reasonable expectation.

For instance, if a Steadman prospect indicated a willingness to give $5 million and had given $3 million before, we could assign a high probability to his or her giving at the $5 million level. If another prospect pointed to the $1 million level, but had given $10,000 only once or twice before, we should assign a very low probability to his or her giving $1 million. If still another prospect pointed to the $10 million level, but had never given before to Steadman or any other organization, we should assume there was little or no chance that he or she would give anywhere close to that level. There may be exceptions to this general rule of thumb, but not enough to them to salvage a flawed campaign.

Clue #7

"The president felt a little skeptical about Marian McGillicuddy, whom he had pegged as a 'piker.' Though she had given for 23 consecutive years, she never gave more than $10,000 at a time … Yet, a few days after that dreaded meeting, she left the president a voicemail saying she would give $1.8 million."

Reasonable Deductions: In fact, Ms. McGillicuddy is the kind of donor who we often overlook. Loyal donors tend to give modest amounts initially and then give much more significantly later in life or through their estates. In assessing campaign potential, officials should pay particularly close attention to those who have given for 10 years or more.

Clue #8

"Further, many of the individuals who had emerged as golden in the wealth screening process were not receptive to visits from anyone from the university, even the president. Those who did agree to meet with the president were polite, but less than forthcoming about their willingness to give. Those who were willing to discuss giving had very strong feelings about what they would support and showed little interest in Steadman's campaign literature or its menu of giving opportunities. After a series of such meetings, the president groused, 'No one is interested in giving to us or meeting our needs; it's all about what they want to achieve.'"

Reasonable Deductions: This should be no surprise. Truly philanthropic people are purpose-driven. They seek out ways to make a difference. In the past, Steadman had failed to identify and engage these constituents. In the intervening years, they developed their own philanthropic objectives, most likely aligning with causes or purposes that resonated with personal experiences and deeply held values.

Steadman officials cannot expect to show up in their lives and say, in effect, "let's talk about what you can do for us." Instead, they must be willing and able to listen and to try to understand the philanthropic path these constituents are on and then determine if it corresponds to something that the university hopes to achieve. If so, the opportunity to align purposes should be explored. But, in one sense, the president of Steadman is right in saying, "No one is interested in meeting our needs." Philanthropy is about meeting societal, not institutional, needs. If Steadman could better articulate how it can influence the world, it would be far better positioned to encourage unaffiliated philanthropists to use the institution to address societal needs of mutual concern.

Clue #9

"Three fundraisers announced their decision to leave, although none had been at Steadman for more than three years."

Reasonable Deductions: While human performance is uneven in every endeavor, it is safe to assume the majority of fundraisers were reasonably able and doing their best. The fact that they had to make 15 or more calls to secure a single appointment with a prospect is the most likely factor contributing to turnover. Staff morale is very difficult to maintain in environments in which workers see a large gap between efforts made and results achieved. Because Steadman previously had done little to reach out to its alumni and other constituents beyond asking for money, receptivity to calls from the university had been in steady decline.

The false expectations of the board, born of wishful thinking and incomplete analyses, in contrast to the reality experienced by the fundraising staff, simply added to the recipe for blame and turnover. Steadman officials would have been far wiser to face the facts and discover why 14 or more prospects were rebuffing fundraisers' requests, and then to become more realistic about what fundraisers could achieve under those circumstances. Increasing the size of the fundraising staff, as the board of Steadman opted to do, was only likely to widen the expect-ation/performance gap.

Clue #10

"Notwithstanding the healthy increases in campaign operations and collateral material, the campaign just seemed like more of the same: the same people giving (albeit more in several surprising cases), the same alumni attending events."

Reasonable Deductions: In most campaigns, approx.-imately 90 percent of the support will come from those who have already given and/or have been long affiliated with the institution. Developing significant levels of support from uninvolved non-givers (who are otherwise philanthropic) takes a long time. Had Steadman done a better job at the outset of articulating agency, however, it would have been better positioned to compete for support from the otherwise philanthropic constituents with whom they had not connected previously.

For instance, had Steadman articulated how it was going to apply its competencies in business and oral history by interviewing the leaders of the top 50 companies in the state, it would have found it relatively easy to engage and eventually attract support from those leaders and other philanthropic entrepreneurs. Or had Steadman projected how it was going to use its distinctive ability in urban ecology to form a coalition of urban partners to develop a plan for a sustainable model of high-quality urban life and then create associated academic programs, it might have attracted the interests of many civic-minded philan-thropists with no previous attachment to the university.

Since it had not articulated ways that non-aligned phil-anthropists could give through Steadman to support their passions, the university should continue to expect to see "the same people." From this perspective, we can see that none of the fingers pointing at the president, consultant, vice president for advancement, or fundraising staff really got to the heart of the matter. While each of these individuals may have had his or her shortcomings, there were far greater issues at play, ones that could not be understood by tactical analysis, but only by stepping back and seeing the strategic and cultural issues at play. The Steadman campaign assumed too much about donor behavior, missed the growing indications of declining appreciation and affiliation, and offered too little explanation of agency—how giving would allow donors to affect the wider world.

KEY TAKEAWAYS

- Myths about fundraising pervade and are often the source of poor campaign performance.

- Fundraising doesn't occur in a vacuum and cannot be reduced to a set of prospects in a gift pyramid. Looking at a field of prospects through the prism of appreciation, affiliation, agency, and accountability will give institutional leaders a much better sense of the strength of constituents' connection to the institution and of the ability of the institution to make a truly effective case for support.

- Institutional leaders need to ensure that campaign goals and projections are rooted in sound analyses and a deep understanding of philanthropic patterns and donor psychology.

- Institutions that have modest or low levels of alumni appreciation and affiliation must make a powerful case for agency in the planning and execution of a comprehensive campaign.

CHAPTER III: PRESIDENT, VP OF ADVANCEMENT, AND BOARD: THE MOST PRODUCTIVE DIVISION OF LABOR

The fictional Steadman case is an example of what can happen when an institution embarks on a campaign without an objective, situational baseline analysis. It is all too easy for any institution to believe it is in a stronger relative position than it, in fact, is or to assume "there's a lot of money out there just for the asking."

Yet launching a comprehensive campaign based on unfounded assumptions will lead to needless expense, frustration, and wasted time. If an institution doesn't root itself in fact, candor, and realism at the outset of the campaign, it will discover that competing expectations and conflicting theories regarding progress will begin to proliferate within the institution and create terrible confusion. In such situations, blame will be assigned, which produces defensiveness and, in turn, a loss of energy and productivity.

Let's explore how this could be avoided and suggest how a more constructive, purposeful trajectory could be forged at the outset of a campaign. The first step requires a clear division of labor among the president, the vice president of advancement, and the board. But each person's responsibilities depend on important feedback from the other constituencies. Here's what they should expect of themselves and each other.

Presidents

Presidents, at the outset of their administration or in the earliest stages of campaign planning, must seek to establish objective, baseline measurements of their institutions' relative and comparative positions—within higher education as well as relative to those specific institutions against which they compete for students, faculty, private support, and other resources. In addition, considerable thought should be given to whom the institution serves and why and how those served perceive the services provided, both short-term and long-term. These kinds of assessments should be used to mark institutional progress in general, but are particularly helpful at the outset of campaigns in helping prospects and donors understand:

- Where is the institution today? Who is it serving? How is it serving students and other key constituents in ways that are not only unique, but relevant to the present and future?

- Where does the institution wish to be in 5, 7, or 10 years? How does it intend to better serve students and other key constituents and thereby make a difference in the community, state, region, nation, or world?

- What specific benchmarks or milestones will it establish to mark progress along the way (and to ensure investors that it is only a disciplined march to a more relevant place)?

Without a beginning, middle and end, an institution will not be effective in drawing donors into a narrative of greater purpose or to sustain the support of loyalists.

Presidential charisma, therefore, is an overrated quality, myths notwithstanding. Philanthropists give to presidents who can articulate where the institution is today, where it needs to go tomorrow, why it is important that it do so, and what it will take to get there. Charisma may be an asset in engaging donors, but a rationale for investment still needs to be established. Donors capable of giving $10 million, for instance, may give an institution one-tenth of that amount because they like the president or enjoy their association with the institution. Inducing them to give more requires specifics as to how additional dollars will yield greater value in some tangible way.

Philanthropists give to presidents who can articulate where the institution is today, where it needs to go tomorrow, why it is important that it do so, and what it will take to get there.

Therefore, the most essential task of a president considering a comprehensive campaign is to lead the effort to re-establish or update the institution's value proposition and to think clearly and courageously about how it can be enhanced by a significant infusion of private support. Many presidents say their institutions need money, sometimes hundreds of millions, if not multiples of those sums. Board members can help presidents and their administrative teams prepare to make a compelling case by first asking how much the institution aspires to raise in a coming campaign, if only a ballpark figure. If the president says $500 million, a board member should pose this question:

> Imagine that we were able to find a donor capable of giving half that amount, a donor who did not presume to tell us how to spend that money, but who insisted that we demonstrate its transformational impact on this institution and those we serve, including setting specific milestones that might be reached in two, five, 10, and 25 years. In others words, what is our plan to convert $250 million into significant and lasting impact?

Responses that sound anything like the following should cause board members concern:

Put it all in endowment

This answer shows a lack of vision, perhaps stemming from a lack of planning. The type of donors most apt to provide large, unrestricted endowments are quintessential insiders, such as long-serving, long- giving board members deeply familiar with the institution's purposes and who have great faith in its agency as a result of their long affiliation with the institution. The trouble is that very few donors fit that description. The rest are interested in achieving specific purposes and making a measurable impact on something that corresponds to their values. This answer does not provide that pathway.

While the rise of the latest entrepreneurial class has produced a remarkable set of philanthropists who have given some of the largest gifts ever, they are not interested in keeping institutions afloat. They often see an endowment as something that protects institutions from reality and adaptability. Before they take part in a philanthropic venture, they expect to see a prospectus that would pass muster from a sharp-eyed venture capitalist.

And had the president in question suggested putting it all in an endowment for student scholarships, the response would only be slightly more satisfactory because the discerning donor would still want answers to the following questions:

- To attract what sorts of students?

- To achieve what institutional or societal ends?

- To encourage what behaviors in the recipients or to obligate them to do what in return?

- Will the relative value (the size of the award relative to the cost of tuition over time) of this endowment be in steady decline without a plan to keep tuition increases within endowment returns?

University leaders must understand that scholarship endowment is the next best thing to unrestricted endowment because the primary use for most unrestricted income and earnings, at most institutions, is to offset a growing demand for financial aid. Since donors are far more likely to endow scholarships than provide unrestricted endowments, campaigns should be designed to offer what donors are most inclined to give to, not just what an institution most wants.

Institutions that have not been committed to, or effective at retaining loyal donors, particularly donors who have given for ten years or more, have very little probability of raising unrestricted endowment. Those institutions without significant contingents of loyal donors would be wise to leave unrestricted endowment off their general campaign menu, but should develop a segmented line of communication and outreach to loyalists with the highest financial capacity and philanthropic propensity, including current and past board members, and long- serving faculty and staff.

Allocate it equally among the deans

This is a distribution plan, not a strategic-investment model. Presidents should know which units, both academic and administrative, are best led and best positioned to convert investments into tangible gains.

Create several endowed chairs so we can attract the best faculty in the world

Discerning philanthropists would want to know which disciplines are the most important and why (enrollment pressures, workforce demands, need for new knowledge, or opportunities for converting faculty knowledge). In addition, money alone does not attract the best faculty. Institutional focus, stature, and purpose do.

Build one or more new buildings

A building is a shell. Donors want to know the purpose and the difference to be made due to the construction. Putting faculty and staff in more commodious and comfortable buildings and giving more people their own offices may improve morale, but donors are interested in productivity. As noted earlier, donors to institutions of higher learning, when presented with a choice of options, have shown less and less interest in capital improvement.

Board members should listen for clearer definitions of purpose based on keener analyses of where a more competitive edge might be honed, where the margin of productivity might be increased, or where there is a real opportunity to deliver greater value to the culture or the economy. Boards can render the best service to their institutions by holding presidents to these standards and, by extension, expecting the presidents to hold their leadership team to the same standards.

And, it is inappropriate for boards to delve deeply into operational detail, they have every right to ask for and receive well-grounded analyses of institutional programs and services that would benefit from larger amounts of private support and the potential constituencies that might be interested in donating such support, from their presidents, vice presidents for advancement and campaign consultants. These analyses will set the stage for effective strategic planning, which is essential to making an effective case for support for a comprehensive campaign.

Vice Presidents of Advancement

Vice presidents of advancement must be prepared to provide objective analyses that address the essential strengths of an institution, particularly those that would be predictive of donor receptivity to campaign goals, including data on the levels of constituent appreciation and affiliation, and how institutional agency can be best expressed to attract the most significant levels of support. They should also be able to project how greater philanthropic capacity can be built through various means of affiliation, including alumni and parent programs, community relations, and business partnerships.

As comprehensive campaign plans take shape, vice presidents of advancement should be able to demonstrate that they have assembled the skill set to not only launch, but also sustain complex operations in the field for a number of years. Board members and presidents should be skeptical of budgetary requests that seek to build advancement heft for the campaign primarily or exclusively through the addition of major gift officers or other fundraising field officers.

A modern comprehensive campaign marches on intelligence and information.

A modern comprehensive campaign marches on intelligence and information. Advanced intelligence is necessary to determine the prospects who are most likely to agree with institutional and campaign purposes. Information is required to sustain thousands of substantive conversations in the field over several years. Sending major gift officers, the most expensive piece of an advancement team, into the field without intelligence or information is wasteful and discouraging for fundraising personnel.

In addition, vice presidents should be very circumspect about the rate of staff growth, even in those instances where boards and presidents are willing to make a far greater investment in advancement and are eager to 'staff up' quickly. A vice president with a total staff of 20, for instance, would be hard pressed to recruit and orient more than 5 new staff members in any given year, and the same percentage would apply to larger opportunities. Growth of more than 20 percent each year can overwhelm support systems, create undo anxiety and turmoil within an operation, and throw too many ill-trained and under-prepared staff at too many under-developed opportunities.

Boards – Governing and Advisory

Board members can best serve the purposes of the campaign by understanding the immense value of leading by example in giving of their time, skills, and resources. Specifically, board members can be extremely useful to presidents and advancement leaders by:

- Serving as sounding boards about the overall purposes of the campaign, particularly its correlation to the strategic direction of the institution;

- Acting like venture capitalists by scrutinizing the draft prospectus to see if the business plan it represents makes sense and is workable;

- Volunteering to participate in the campaign initiative that best corresponds to their passions and areas of expertise so that they will be natural advocates and supporters; and

- Preserving and enhancing relationships with current major and loyal donors. There's no better stewardship than board members calling donors to ask how they are feeling about their past investments to understand what their future ones might look like.

When boards, presidents, and vice presidents for advancement work in common purpose, campaign goals can be achieved more expeditiously. Yet common purpose is not merely a matter of good intention or even expressed commitments. It's a matter of getting the generals looking at the same map at the same time. And the map for a comprehensive campaign must be built on best practices in strategic planning and fundraising. These are evidence-based fields, with conclusions drawn from data.

Board members should commit to putting aside their assumptions and theories about fundraising and join with the president and advancement staff in a collective search for the best way to realize the potential of their institution, given its unique characteristics and circumstances. Comparing fundraising totals from various institutions, or the investments made in them will yield little insight, much less the basis for decision making, if taken out of the context of their particular institution and its current and potential donor base.

Institutional leaders should realize that formulaic strategies such as "let's just get everyone to give $25" have been tried over and over and have resulted in consistently resounding failure. Whether the amount sought is $1 or $1,000, this approach has never succeeded for long because most people are motivated by their purposes, not your fundraising totals. If people are inclined to give $1 or $1,000, they will direct it to their favorite cause, not to an organization that implores them to give that amount so that the organization can reach its fundraising goal.

Further, as reviews of numerous donor records show, people will give at a level that they deem appropriate—

given their income, values, and the relative importance they assign to an organization—not what an organization suggests they should give. And, finally, campaigns that seek to convince lots of people to give small amounts are acting like a charity, which diminishes philanthropic response and potential. The evidence – the largest gifts given to most institutions of higher learning over the past two decades – suggests overwhelmingly that it is far more productive to project a great purpose and demonstrate how it can be realized through the bundling of gifts of all sizes. In that way, even the most modest investors can be a part of a great achievement.

At the outset of campaigns, board members could render the most valuable service by helping their presidents define not what donors can do for the institution, but rather what the institution can do for the community or society. Calling for vision statements and elevator pitches minimizes the challenge and opportunity ahead. Major gifts are brokered over the course of 18 to 21 months and through multiple, substantive exchanges between a prospect and an institutional representative.

The quality of the concepts that an institution advances in a campaign, the authenticity with which they are delivered, and the reciprocity of purposes they seek to achieve have everything to do with the quality of prospects that an institution attracts.

KEY TAKEAWAYS

- The president, board chair, and vice president of advancement have critical roles that each must play well in advance of a campaign to ensure that it yields lasting strategic gains.

- The president must lead a thorough, objective assessment of an institution's strengths and weaknesses vis-à-vis its peers and the markets it serves.

- Boards must make sure those assessments are objective and be willing to challenge assumptions about institutional direction that are naïve or self-serving.

- Presidents must have not just a general sense of how much they want to raise, but also be able to articulate the transformative impact that amount will have on the institution and those it serves.

- Vice presidents of advancement should have not a fundraising plan to secure support from the most obvious prospects, but rather a plan to develop deep constituent engagement throughout the campaign and beyond to create a richer pipeline of affiliated, purpose- driven prospects.

- Boards should help create a strategic, evidence-based culture by objectively asking, "Why are we taking this approach? What evidence do we have that it is the best way? How will we measure success and at what intervals of time?"

CHAPTER IV: IMAGINING AND IMPLEMENTING BETTER WAYS

Using Steadman as a foil, we can begin to imagine a better way of determining if an institution has sufficient strengths, and in the right areas, to consider moving forward with the planning of a comprehensive campaign. Critical factors to consider include the following:

Donor Pipeline	Annual alumni participation
	Large quotient of loyal donors
Depth of Affiliation	Well-developed networks of alumni and other constituents
	Strategic engagement of volunteers
Agency	True strategic planning
	Service orientation
Institutional Inflection Point	When an institution's offerings and capabilities are what the world is demanding

Since these will be critical to helping readers evaluate their own institution's potential, each is described in more detail in the following pages.

Donor Pipeline

According to *U.S. News & World Report*, the colleges and universities with the highest percentages of annual alumni giving are as follows:

FIGURE 1

Princeton University (NJ)	62.9%
Thomas Aquinas College (CA)	58.3%
Williams College (MA)	56.9%
Florida College	54.4% 54 (tie)
Bowdoin College (ME)	54.2%
Middlebury College (VT)	53%
Davidson College (NC)	52.9%
Wellesley College (MA)	51.4%
Carleton College (MN)	50.6%
Amherst College (MA)	49.2%

Source: US News College Compass. This data is accurate as of October 20, 2015.

Annual Alumni Participation

The percentage of alumni giving back to their alma mater is an important baseline measure in assessing an institution's ability to stage a successful campaign. Since approximately one-third of Americans give to one or more organizations every year (another 42 percent will give occasionally, and another 25 percent will give very rarely or never), institutions of higher learning that have done a reasonably good job of engendering appreciation and promoting affiliation should be able to sustain annual alumni giving rates of 33 percent or more, or to map against the larger societal patterns.

The levels of annual alumni participation in Figure 1 suggest exceptional levels of appreciation and affiliation, if not agency. Note in Figure 1 that academic distinction, as measured in the right-hand column according to where an institution stands in its U.S. News classification (for example, "National Liberal Arts" or "National Universities"), is not a predictor of alumni participation. The fact that Thomas Aquinas is ranked 61st among national liberal arts colleges has not prevented that institution from instilling high levels of student and alumni loyalty.

In fact, over-reliance on marketing academic distinction and under- reliance on building alumni affiliation is one of the reasons that annual alumni giving has been declining for 20 straight years and why, today, fewer than one in 10 alumni are giving back annually to their alma mater. Too many institutions have pointed to their declining levels of alumni participation as a part of a national trend, but what other alumni from other institutions do should not affect how your alumni feel about your institution.

In fact, over-reliance on marketing academic distinction and under-reliance on building alumni affiliation is one of the reasons that annual alumni giving has been declining for 20 straight years and why, today, fewer than one in 10 alumni are giving back annually to their alma mater.

Institutions contemplating comprehensive campaigns need to begin by assessing the depth of alumni appreciation, and not just in broad ways. Many alumni will say they received an excellent or very good education and express ongoing pride in their alma mater. That does not mean they will give. In general, several other factors must be in place. The alumni will have to be philanthropic in general, feel a sense of personal indebtedness to one or more people on the faculty or staff, and believe that the value of their degree exceeded the cost. These, then, are the precise lines of inquiry that an institution must explore in alumni surveys, whether they are conducted face-to-face, online, or over the phone.

Appreciation levels expressed by other constituents, including parents, as well as corporations and businesses that hire graduates, also should be assessed. Parents' appreciation tends to be short-lived, often peaking after admission or the first time their child comes home with a positive report or crows about grades. It tends to wane by the end of the sophomore year, when it is assumed that the child is halfway to self-sufficiency or the parents are halfway to freedom from tuition payments.

The level of appreciation among corporations and businesses can be assessed by conducting an inventory of interactions that includes the following questions:

- Have they given previously? If so, are they satisfied with their return on investment?

- Do they provide internships for students? Has the number been increasing?

- Do they hire graduates? Has the number been increasing?

- Do they sponsor research at the institution? Have the levels changed in recent years?

- Do they sponsor athletics?

- Are they vendors? Is the institution becoming a larger or smaller client?

- Are alumni on their boards or in senior executive positions?

The more of these interactions, the greater the likelihood of campaign support, especially if the request depicts how the alliance between parties can be made more strategic and productive. Businesses and corporations don't give out of the goodness of their hearts; they give to realize corporate objectives. And there's nothing the matter with that if they align with and prove to be synergistic with institutional objectives.

Quotient of Loyal Donors

The volume of donors, alumni or otherwise, who have given to your institution for 10 years or more is the single best metric in determining an institution's campaign potential. Nothing is more predictive of how many people might give, and at what level, in a campaign than the number of people who have already given at various levels. In most cases, this volume is waning with each passing decade.

Alumni who graduated before 1980 have a much greater tendency to be loyal donors (10 consecutive years or more) than those who graduated in the 1980s who, in turn, are more inclined to be loyal than those who graduated in the 1990s. This is not just because of their age, but because of generational behaviors. Boomers, and those who preceded them, have demonstrated greater loyalty to institutions, including to employers, churches and causes. Those who followed, most especially Millennials, are far more likely to be loyal to causes than to institutions, again a pattern that is reflected in their employment and their philanthropic affiliations.

Figure 2, part of an analysis of an institution's philanthropic potential, reveals an all-too-typical situation. It represents the number of donors who have given for 10 years or more by decade of graduation. The declines in the 1980s, 1990s, and 2000s are symptomatic of phenomena discussed earlier, including rising tuition; increases in tuition-related debt (especially in the number of indebted graduates, not the average debt); fewer job opportunities; coupled with and, in some cases, exacerbated by, more intensive and constant institutional fundraising requests; and other factors that have caused many alumni to say, "My alma mater does little to reach out to me beyond asking for money."

FIGURE 2: ANNUAL GIVING IN EACH OF THE PAST 10 FISCAL YEARS (FY 03 - FY 12), BY DECADE OF GRADUATION

DECADE	# OF ALUMNI
1930	9
1940	207
1950	641
1960	512
1970	444
1980	336
1990	183
2000	29

When reading the chart in Figure 2, institutional leaders must keep several important facts in mind:

- The alumni of the 1950s, 1960s, and 1970s who became loyal donors began giving shortly after graduation and formed a lifelong habit.

- If alumni don't begin giving regularly shortly after graduation, the probability of their giving decreases with every passing year; they form other philanthropic habits (supporting causes other than their alma mater), which become more entrenched over time.

- The probability of reversing the trend evinced by those who graduated in the 1990s and 2000s is small.

- The pipeline of future major gifts and estate gifts, as a result, has diminished significantly for institutions with similar giving patterns.

Depth of Affiliation

Well-developed Alumni Networks

If a significant depth of appreciation can be found across constituencies, particularly within and among alumni, the prospects of a campaign brighten considerably. However, even grateful alumni who believe that the value of their degree was far greater than the cost are less likely to give or will give much less than they are capable of if they have not been recently affiliated with their alma maters. The more recent and substantive the alumni affiliation, the greater the probability of significant giving throughout the life of the campaign.

Strategic Engagement of Volunteers

The quality and quantity of constituent engagement should be assessed objectively before a campaign is launched. Key questions include:

- How many constituents are currently volunteering? How many are engaged on campus? How many are involved around the state, region, country, and beyond?

- What is the quality of these volunteers? Are we capturing the talents of our most accomplished constituents?

- Are our volunteer opportunities substantive? Do we allow volunteers to make significant and lasting contributions?

- Have we created too many advisory boards, largely because we think it will cause the participants to give?

- Do we spend most of our time at those meetings touting our successes?

- Are the board members actually doing anything other than listening?

- Are they reducing the institution's workload and improving the quality of its services or are they increasing its workload and expenses?

- How does the alumni association measure its effectiveness?

- How do the parents' program or other constituent-engagement programs measure their effectiveness? Do we see a powerful correlation between constituent engagement and giving?

- Do we have a strategic volunteer-engagement plan? What skill sets might we systematically identify and engage for institutional gain? Are we using volunteers in innovative ways? Is volunteer engagement a path to creating a more sustainable economic model for the institution?

Of particular and growing importance is the development of a volunteer management plan. Since volunteers give 10 times more than non-volunteers, the recruiting, empaneling, and empowering of the right volunteers, particularly before and at the outset of a campaign will have a significant impact on major gift productivity – if the right volunteers are chosen and if they are engaged in substantive tasks that call upon their skills and experiences. By the same token, ill- chosen volunteers who are slotted into advisory boards with ill- defined purposes and goals, will prove to be a significant drain on the time, talent, and budget of the advancement staff. A realistic plan, projecting where volunteers, possessed of specific skills, can make a specific impact on the institution is of immense value. That same plan should also acknowledge which volunteers and volunteer activities are falling short of reasonable expectation, and what can be done to sunset low-functioning advisory boards and/or redirect the best volunteers on those boards to more productive activities.

This volunteer plan should seek to create or enhance a "farm system" of volunteer recruit-

ment and development, one in which the most able volunteers are recognized, rewarded and moved into higher levels of responsibility, and, ultimately to positions on the institution's foundation board or governing board.

This volunteer plan should seek to create or enhance a "farm system" of volunteer recruitment and development, one in which the most able volunteers are recognized, rewarded and moved into higher levels of responsibility, and, ultimately to positions on the institution's foundation board or governing board. Indeed, many a campaign falters because members of the "highest board" were not thoroughly vetted, or expected to prove themselves in other capacities, including giving, before being elevated to those positions.

The consequences of low appreciation and weak affiliation can be seen in Figure 3 which shows the results of an actual alumni survey done at a private university. The responses suggest relatively weak alumni respect and affiliation and, therefore, little basis for pursuing a comprehensive campaign.

High levels of constituent appreciation coupled with considerable, substantive, and strategic affiliation would suggest an institution has the fundamental strengths to explore a significant campaign. Indeed, if an institution has significant appreciation and affiliation, it can run a campaign to achieve broad purposes—student support, faculty support, capital improvements—but it would be strengthened further with a greater emphasis on agency and accountability. With strong levels of appreciation and broad-based affiliation, an institution also can run a campaign of implied agency: "You know what we did for you (and, perhaps, your children and grandchildren), and you know what we do day in and day out, so help us continue to do a great job."

FIGURE 3: SAMPLE ALUMNI SURVEY

Middle Tier Ratings

	Describe Completely	Describe Completely/ Very Well
Has state of the art facilities	24%	56%
Is an excellent educational institution	23%	65%
Has many successful alumni	22%	64%
Provides students with practical, real-world skills	21%	64%
Has an ethnicity-diverse student body	21%	55%
Has faculty who take a personal interest in student's success	20%	57%
Displays a strong sense of values and ethics	19%	60%
Is politically connected	18%	50%
Has small class sizes	17%	48%
Has supportive environment that helps students thrive	19%	55%
Is progressive	14%	52%
Is community-oriented	14%	51%
Values its relationship with alumni by keeping them closely connected	14%	45%
Does a good job preparing students for a competitive job market	13%	48%
Has flexible policies and programs to help students reach their goals	13%	46%
Average Rating	17%	50%

Agency

Agency, or the ability to project with some precision, how donors, by funding a particular initiative or program, can give **through** an institution of higher learning to achieve a measurable impact on the human condition at a local, regional, national, or global level. Examples of agency include:

- $350 million given by the Chan family in 2014 through Harvard's School of Public Health to slow or reverse four global health threats.

- $400 million given in 2016 by Phil Knight through Stanford to "recruit graduate students around the globe to address society's most intractable problems, including poverty and climate change," according to the New York Times.

- $10 million given by Mary Bucksbaum and Patrick Scanlan in 2016 to the University of Iowa to create a STEAM (Science, Technology, Engineering, Arts and Math) Academy for high achieving 10th graders.

An institution's ability to conceive where and how it can demonstrate the greatest agency is an enormous advantage in contemplating, conceiving, planning, and executing the most effective of all comprehensive campaigns—ones that are both institution-building and society-serving and that incorporate the essential symbiosis between the two.

Most institutions, for a variety of reasons, do not find themselves these days with an abundance of appreciative, previously unasked, or hoping- to-be asked constituents. Indeed, the apparent success of so many campaigns in the past few decades has caused many higher education leaders, sometimes with the assent of fundraising consultants, to pooh-pooh the importance of alumni programs and other means of constituent affiliation. As a result, an institution with 100,000 alumni is apt to have fewer than 3,000 of them engaged in substantive, meaningful volunteer work or critical activity. Very few institutions can boast of alumni or constituent programs that have resulted in more than 5 percent of their alumni giving 10 hours or more of service in any given year.

Further, many institutions with long-standing, if relatively modest, alumni programs and other constituent-engagement activities have not optimized the means of affiliation available. Too many offer only traditional or "rah-rah" events that seem to assume that alumni are boosters-in-waiting, eager to lap up the latest good news from their alma mater or generally to cheer it on.

Many institutions rely on advisory boards as their principal means of engaging alumni and other key constituents, but use the board meetings to impress those in attendance with all the good things that are happening at the university, college, or school. This is done in the mistaken belief that the more positive information thrust at constituents, the more impressed they will be and the more likely they will be to give. Yet this approach can produce the opposite of the intended effect. Advisory board members may be asking, "If everything is so great, why do they need us? Is there no important work for us to do?"

The purpose of encouraging constituents to feel a sense of affiliation with an institution, therefore, is not to celebrate but to find means of working together to advance the mission of the institution in measurable and lasting ways. The best volunteers are busy, accomplished people who become engaged not because they want to be informed or entertained, but because they want to make a measurable and lasting impact for a cause or purpose that resonates with their deepest values. Volunteers give 10 times more than non-engaged philanthropists, but their probability of doing so can be greatly diminished by offering them inconsequential or uninteresting volunteer opportunities.

Similarly, the philanthropic potential of volunteer positions will not be optimized if important duties are offered to people who are not innately philanthropic or civically oriented.

The best form of affiliation is that which allows for individual values to be channeled through institutional purposes for societal gain. Indeed, this is what an adept comprehensive campaign achieves on a large scale.

Institutions with low levels of affiliation cannot expect to achieve success in a comprehensive campaign if they do not understand and seek to harness the power of agency—to reawaken residual appreciation, create the means of powerful, widespread affiliation, and attract purpose-driven philanthropists who have not been previously aligned with them.

The two most powerful ways available to attract purpose-driven philanthropists and grant them agency in a shared future are:

1. Involve alumni in ***true strategic planning***.

2. Adopt a ***true service orientation*** that your campaign will articulate and fulfill.

True Strategic Planning

No end of activities can be subsumed under the rubric of strategic planning. A true strategic planning process, however, should be a rigorous effort to determine, in the most objective, least self-serving manner, how an institution's assets relate to external opportunities and threats and how those assets might be reshaped and presented to capitalize on the former and avoid the latter. It is the means of bringing healthy doses of reality, derived from listening to key constituencies and studying larger socio-economic trends, to the shaping of internal aspirations.

True strategic planning must recognize the one constant——change. No organization can afford to do the same thing over and over, no matter how well it might have worked in the past.

Since true strategic planning is essential to the demonstration of agency, and since demonstrable agency is so important to the framing of a compelling case for support, board members must insist on rigorous strategic planning as a prerequisite to launching a comprehensive campaign and must do all they can to ensure that it is rooted in fact, not wishful thinking.

Given these facts, then, the role of the board is to determine if:

- A rigorous and objective assessment of the institution's financial health can be conducted (using an established formula like the Composite Financial Index that will allow for a comparative analysis);

- There is a broad-based understanding within the institution of its relative financial position;

- There is a commitment to exploring difficult decisions to preserve or strengthen the viability of the institution; and

- There is a planning process underway to reallocate resources to preserve and enhance essential strengths.

If the board determines that these elements exist (recognizing that there will never be a perfect consensus), an institution can begin thinking in earnest about a comprehensive campaign, knowing that it is in a position to convert new investment into greater institutional strength and avoid using it to temporarily compensate for underlying weakness.

If these elements don't exist or are uncertain, boards should resist or check any attempt to launch a campaign as a rescue effort. A need- based campaign, particularly one launched by a struggling institution, fails to understand the dynamics of philanthropy. Increasingly, even the most committed and loyal supporters are questioning whether their giving is going toward excellence or survival. They are questioning whether the institution has done all it could to eliminate waste, tighten its belt, pursue greater efficiencies, and reallocate resources from faltering programs to productive ones. And they are questioning whether institutions are fundraising to avoid making difficult decisions.

Faculty Input in Strategic Planning

Issues of shared governance and academic freedom can and will play out in the planning and execution of comprehensive campaigns. If anything, the comprehensive campaign of the future will need greater faculty presence— in setting academic direction, shaping campaign content, lending intellectual heft to campaign events and communications, and engaging larger numbers of alumni and stakeholders in more satisfying ways. Indeed, it is the lasting bonds between faculty members and former students that mark the strongest philanthropic cultures in higher education.

The greater the integration of effort and cohesion among the faculty, administration, and board at the outset and throughout the campaign, the more the institution will be able to sustain substantive conversations with its stakeholders and, in so doing, potentially secure larger financial commitments. There is little utility in board members disparaging elements of a faculty culture that are well-established and deeply prized, or being too confrontational about long-established practices and policies.

While almost everyone understands that there are indeed ways in which higher education should be "run more like a business," there are a growing number of businesses that have become highly successful by emulating higher-education practices, including putting a premium on brainpower, emphasizing the value of research as the path to product development, creating conditions that allow employees to innovate through cross-collaboration, and encouraging a wide variety of personal expression to create a culture that can look at an issue in many different ways.

When it comes to matters like strategic planning, formulating a case for support, and framing white papers and proposals to lend depth and dimension to fundraising efforts, the strengths and weaknesses of academic culture will become obvious to trustees. For example, the process may seem unduly long and layered with numerous meetings, perhaps several town halls in which seemingly endless testimony is elicited, reviews by various committees, and the circulation of drafts. To the business mind, it may seem like long-windedness and indecision— until one considers that true scholarship, the bedrock of academic distinction and lasting impact, is a deliberate, painstaking, iterative, often collaborative search for significant, substantive, and seminal knowledge.

True scholarship is a commitment to drawing careful inferences from massive amounts of knowledge or data. If faculty members are involved in a planning process, and well they should be, they will approach the task as scholars and apply the principles that have brought them distinction in their respective fields. While that will prolong the process, it will yield results that have credibility and ownership internally, and therefore increase the potential of external sustainability. Board members cannot afford to forget the power of disaffected faculty members, especially the longest serving and most influential, in swaying alumni opinion.

Many faculty members fail to understand that most private support will come from people who have been shaped by cultures very different than their own—cultures that teach lessons, sometimes hard ones, about the forces of change and shifting market imperatives that sweep away once-successful businesses and enterprises with astonishing speed. Strategic planning left entirely or largely to the faculty often produces documents that are broadly aspirational and somewhat platitudinous about academic values and the pursuit of excellence. These documents may focus on the refinement of processes (for example, institutional decision making, fostering interdisciplinary research, fostering civility, or workload issues), rather than on where to focus resources for the greater good of the organization, how to locate and reduce waste or inefficiencies, or how to establish performance measures or outcomes.

Boards can help their presidents by pushing back on unrealistic faculty expectations and the inability to make hard choices, and by preparing the culture for a comprehensive campaign by previewing the concerns and objections that are likely to surface when academic aspirations meet donor expectations.

Outside Analysis

In considering a comprehensive campaign, the board should insist on an objective, data-rich analysis of outside forces and factors that will present both opportunities and threats, especially those that will affect the institution's most significant supply lines. That research, which may need to be done by, or at least reviewed by, an outside firm with experience in data-driven analyses, should be presented in the form of trend analysis and include the opinions and attitudes of those the institution serves and those to whom the institution will turn for support.

The institutions that listen most closely to their key constituents and hold "objective mirrors" up to themselves maintain an ongoing strategic mindset that mitigates, if not obviates, the disjuncture between internal expectations and external realities. While constituent research can be expensive, it generally costs less than the annual salary of a major gift officer. Further, that research will allow all gift officers to work more effectively and the institution to run a more cost-effective campaign.

Key constituents, of course, include students and their parents, and in the strategic-planning process. Boards should ask what systems, structures, and ongoing listening devices have been put in place to understand the following:

- How are we perceived by prospective students vis-à-vis our peers?

- Why do we not enroll a portion of the best students we admit? What others campuses are they most apt to attend?

- How do students and parents feel about their first interactions and transitions into our campus community?

- How do our student retention rates compare to other institutions?

- Which of our incoming students are most at risk and what are we doing to monitor their progress so we can intervene in a timely manner?

- Do students see us living up to the promises made in our recruitment literature after the first quarter or semester? After the first and second year?

- Do graduating seniors believe that the value of their education exceeded the cost? Do they see themselves as lifelong adherents of our institution?

- How many newly minted graduates re-engage with the institution and give meaningfully of their time, talent, and treasure?

- What do recent graduates (within 10 years) believe was the most and least valuable part of the educational experience? Who or what stands out most positively or negatively?

- How do midlife (11 to 28 years since graduation), mature (29 to 45 years out), and senior alumni (46+ years out) respond to the same questions?

- How have graduates' perceptions of, and investment in, the alma mater changed over the decades?

- How do internship providers rate the quality of our students vis-à-vis those from other institutions?

- Who are the greatest employers of our alumni, and what is their perception of the quality of the graduates we produce?

- How do prospective students view the correlations between our degree programs and their future employability? How do current students feel about those issues? Recent grads?

A deeper and ongoing understanding of these issues and the relationship between student life and alumni affiliation and between alumni affiliation and alumni giving are essential to creating a strategic mindset—one that corrects the future course by learning from the past. If the institution is one where annual alumni giving has been in decline and fewer donors are giving for 10 or more years, the questions listed above should help organizations understand where their value proposition is breaking down.

It makes little sense, for instance, to expend significant efforts or sums of money on wooing alumni who feel the institution didn't keep its promises, afford them enough personal attention, deliver an education that was commensurate with the cost, do enough to help them find a job, or reach out to them as alumni beyond asking for money. An institution can only go so far forward without reconciling the past.

The Steadman example earlier raised the question of why so few alumni prospects were receptive to fundraisers' calls, but, in that sense, our fictional university is not unusual. Many fundraisers at many institutions make 20 or more calls (or send emails) to secure a single appointment. Before launching a campaign, it would behoove institutions to know what their call-to-appointment ratio is and to discover the larger cultural reasons for low response levels. Imposing more rigorous performance measures on fundraisers in such situations will only drive up the rate of staff turnover and do little, if anything, to ameliorate the underlying issues.

True Service Orientation

The tone an institution sets in its campaign communications is of immense importance. Institutions that
achieve the highest levels of agency do so with the greatest
conscious determination to serve. Their leaders seek to
create a stronger ethos of service to humanity.

The pursuit of institutional status—whether it is increased
student selectivity, higher rankings, more prominent
professors, or elusive claims of "excellence"—makes for a
much less effective case for support.

While institutional status or a more competitive posture
may appeal to some alumni, we know the real drivers of
philanthropic actions are personal values and personal
experiences. Institutions that project how they are seeking
to address larger societal issues—be it the remediation of
diseases, the expansion of entrepreneurial innovation,
greater understanding among cultures, or advances in
social justice—attract the attention and support of
passionate, purpose-driven philanthropists who see the
opportunity to exercise their personal values.

The vast majority of four-year institutions, for instance,
refer to their mission as tripartite—teaching, research and
public service, yet few have a vice president for public
service, a strategic service plan, or can even boast of a
complete inventory of all the service work being done by
the faculty, staff and students. Service, therefore, is left
largely to individual volition—yet, in many, many
instances, the quality, array and relevance of service work
being done by faculty, notwithstanding little or no
recognition and even less financial support from their
administrations, is quite remarkable.

Yet for all the emphasis that higher education places on
community service, few institutions actually record,

quantify, promote, and perpetuate it. Imagine an institution, for example, distinguished by the large number of graduates who commit two years of their lives to Teach for America (TFA). The institution may take great pride in that fact and a certain amount of credit for admitting students with a strong inclination to serve others and/or creating conditions that deepened students' desire to improve the human condition.

Yet, all too often, the institution brags about the good work being done by its graduates, but does not reengage them. The Teach for America (TFA) experience, however, often proves life changing. Many who charge into inner city or disadvantaged schools are appalled by what they find. As a result, many TFA alumni commit themselves to school reform, either by creating alternative or charter schools themselves, or by working as volunteers within the system or the community to bring about change.

The institution that only brags about its students' two years in TFA, but does not use that service to reengage them misses a great opportunity to achieve a commonality of purpose with some of its most impressive young alumni, who are likely to make a difference in society throughout their lives. A wiser institution might, for example, invite its TFA alumni to a summit on school reform, which would allow them to share their experiences, impart the lessons they have learned, and advocate for specific changes. In so doing, it would reengage exemplary alumni and validate the dedication and direction of their lives.

Institutions add depth and dimension to their campaigns by featuring ways that faculty service efforts can be enhanced through private support. For instance, some institutional leaders might consider creating an umbrella organization, perhaps an Institute for Social Innovation, in which the volunteer work done by faculty could be inventoried, coordinated, and evaluated as to impact. Donors might be interested in creating such an initiative, providing seed funding for promising initiatives, providing grants for teams of faculty and students to work on critical community needs, or to provide specific services identified by a community needs assessment.

These efforts could be further complemented and enriched if institutions of higher learning developed the means to assess and coordinate community service being done by alumni, or to invite alumni to participate in service learning projects, which we will explore later in this book.

An institution can strengthen its fundraising potential in advance of a campaign by assessing the state of public service at an institution and reflecting if:

- Teaching and research can be strengthened by a closer linkage and commitment to public service,

- Student recruitment and student life can be made more attractive and memorable by efforts to implement classroom lessons in such a way that they benefit the community, or if the classroom lessons can be enriched by learning directly from community or nonprofit leaders,

- Higher quotients of alumni could be engaged in the life of the institution, and thereby reverse the trend of declining alumni participation experienced by most institutions, by matching alumni community service passions with those of the faculty and or staff and students,

- A greater sense of share institutional values can be realized through the aforementioned strategies, and, of course, if

- Greater private support can be secured by projecting this kind of vision.

Institutional Inflection Point

Another criterion for boards to consider in weighing the workability of a campaign is the *inflection moment*—when offerings and capabilities of an institution appear to be exactly what the outside world is demanding. This might manifest itself in many ways, including combinations of the following:

- Positive enrollment patterns;

- Alumni achieving high levels of employment in good jobs and admission to top graduate schools;

- Increasing demand for graduates in fields for which the institution is known;

- High levels of annual alumni participation (with increases in donors and dollars);

- A president and leadership team who are well received by alumni, parents, and other key constituents; and

- Growing success in securing governmental grants.

The confluence of many of these circumstances is ideal for the launch of a comprehensive campaign because evidence of institutional success is so tangible; the beneficiaries of the institutional experience are obviously grateful; it is so easy to show that the institution is providing just what the external world demands; and it would be relatively easy to show how increases in private support could be converted to greater societal contribution. Yet very few institutions can boast of all of these phenomena. The Steadman example is more the norm.

Given the demographic realities of the day and the enrollment challenges that will persist for at least the next decade, institutions considering comprehensive campaigns must give much greater consideration—in their strategic planning and in the framing of their case for support—to how private support can attract, retain, and ensure the success of more students. Indeed, the relative dearth of students in most parts of the country, the decline in average family income over the past decade, and the need to reduce the cost of education, including by finding the means for students to graduate in four years, present colleges with the opportunity to distinguish themselves by seeking funding for innovative ways to meet these challenges.

Once again, true strategic planning is the means by which institutional competencies are reshaped and refined to meet external challenges and opportunities. Similarly, institutions that ignore these realities and urge constituents to continue to give to expensive, but ineffective programs stand little chance of engendering significant support.

KEY TAKEAWAYS

- The four key factors that must be fully assessed in advance of a comprehensive campaign are the strength of the donor pipeline, the depth of constituent affiliation, the institution's ability to demonstrate greater agency through selected philanthropic investments, and the momentum of the institution.

- Institutions are witnessing, with every passing decade, a greater loss in the volume of loyal (10 years or more of giving) alumni, the source of most major and estate gifts.

- More attention and resources should be focused on building meaningful volunteer structures and constituent depth to ensure a stronger community of shared purposes and greater receptivity to institutional fundraising requests.

- An exceptional case for support is rooted in true strategic planning, which, in turn, is rooted in institutional soul-searching about whether its relevance is waxing or waning, and how it can do a better job of demonstrating agency.

- If the evidence suggests that an institution is at an inflection point, a comprehensive campaign can be highly catalytic.

CHAPTER V: ADAPTING TO NEW REALITIES

The new realities and the varied ways they are affecting institutions call into question the generic comprehensive campaign of the past few decades. The hallmarks of the generic campaign include the following:

- A seven- to 10-year timeframe;

- A feasibility study to determine the level of support available for broad institutional purposes;

- Sizing the institution's needs to the campaign total;

- Stating the institution's needs in broad terms so as to accommodate as many internal stakeholders as possible;

- Campaigning in a "quiet phase" until 50 percent of the campaign total is secured;

- Increasing the size of the frontline fundraising staff to reach larger swaths of prospects;

- Insignificant investment in building stronger constituent relations;

- Expending significant sums on campaign launch activities and collateral material;

- Emphasizing the dollar goal as the primary objective;

- Accounting by categories (for example, how much money was raised for financial aid, faculty support, programmatic initiatives, and capital improvements);

- Considerable emphasis on capital improvements; and

- Emphasizing the "triple ask"—giving concurrently to the annual fund, the campaign, and making an estate commitment.

The New Campaign Realities

The new realities, however, seem to call for consideration of a very different kind of comprehensive campaign with greater emphasis on the following:

Setting mission milestones and goals for societal impact, not just dollar goals and broad priorities

Donors don't wake up in the morning asking, "How can I give away more money?" The most conscientious ask, "How can I make a difference that needs to be made?" or "How can I pass on the most important lessons that life has taught me?" Institutions struggling with declining alumni participation and/or a loss of donors won't win them back by stressing the importance of dollars received. Instead, as discussed above, they need to focus on higher purposes to be served. The traditional campaign is sized to "how much is out there" based on past giving and predictive analytics. The better way is to ask, "How can we exercise greater agency in selected areas? Do those areas correspond with known philanthropic interests? How much would it take to achieve ambitious purpose-driven goals, and what is the probability of securing the necessary resources?"

> *Donors don't wake up in the morning asking, "How can I give away more money?" The most conscientious ask, "How can I make a difference that needs to be made?" or "How can I pass on the most important lessons that life has taught me?"*

Over-emphasizing dollar goals and under-emphasizing agency make for a bland case and causes an institution to appeal once again to   its known donors, most of them 60 years of age or older. While past giving is the best predictor of future giving, institutions must concern themselves with strategies that attract more young donors and encourage loyal giving so that there will be enough "past giving" to call upon in the future. Finally, many campaigns have met their dollar goals, but fallen short of various campaign categories or specific initiatives. However, when donors hear that institutions have met or exceeded their dollar goals, they assume all their objectives have been met and, therefore, see no immediate need for additional investments of private support.

Constituent research and field testing

Too much emphasis has been placed on traditional analytics, including the creation of gift pyramids, prioritized prospect lists, and prospect rating systems—all of which assume certain things about donor behavior, including strength of affiliation and level of expected generosity—that depend too much on speculation from development staff and others within the organization and too little on hard evidence. To achieve higher levels of effectiveness and economy, the comprehensive campaign of the future will require more rigorous scrubbing of those assumptions. This will entail more painstaking reviews of previous philanthropy at all levels, better assessments of the competition for prospects' loyalties, and more sophisticated readings of the personal and values-based factors driving donor behavior.

Focus on a shorter duration between donors' giving and seeing the impact

The trend is undeniable. Donors want to see impact. A campaign designed to show how gifts can be converted into quantifiable outcomes in one, three, and five years will resonate with purpose-driven donors. A campaign need be no longer than it takes to raise money for the purposes defined. Comprehensive campaigns have grown increasingly longer to achieve one thing: increasing the campaign goal. That total may offer institutional bragging rights, but it does not promote giving, particularly if the institution does not relate the amounts raised to specific outcomes. The greater the demonstrable impact and the sooner it can be documented, the better donors will feel about their investment and the more they will adhere to and affiliate with the institution.

A campaign designed to show how gifts can be converted into quantifiable outcomes in one, three, and five years will resonate with purpose-driven donors.

Less emphasis on moving from a quiet phase to the public phase based on the percentage of dollars raised

A campaign of shorter duration and with more emphasis on mission milestones still needs to be previewed and tested with the institution's most promising prospects, but the decision to move ahead would be based on donor receptivity and early investment in those objectives, not on a particular dollar amount. In other words, the institution would go ahead with the objectives that had strong support and would withdraw from, or perhaps redesign, those that did not.

More front-end intelligence and constituency building

As discussed above, the vast majority of gifts given in a comprehensive campaign come from those who have previously given to the institution and who have served in significant volunteer capacities. Further, many donors don't give because an institution is in a campaign, but because it gives them an opportunity to give to a part of the institution or to a program or initiative that resonates with their values. That is why more and more donors are designating their gifts for specific purposes; they care more about art or medicine or science or engineering than they do about the broad purposes of the institution. Therefore, it is wise to spend a great deal of time listening and paying attention to what donors and other constituents care about and exploring how their passions align with institutional competencies and purposes, and then designing a campaign that allows for interests to be aligned and common goals to be pursued.

Proceeding in this manner allows institutions to promote and sustain higher levels of constituent affiliation. A greater investment in front- end intelligence would allow an institution to deploy its gift officers, the most expensive part of an advancement operation, with more qualified leads and information that is more apt to resonate with those leads. Gift officers would not be used to cold call or develop leads from speculatively selected prospects. Additional development staff would be hired only when there were more well developed leads than could be responded to.

High-content but understated supporting materials

Discerning donors question expenditures that do not directly advance the purposes of the institution. They struggle to reconcile an institution's claim that it needs money, sometimes for very elemental purposes, with the evidence that it is spending on non-essential functions. Furthermore, expensive, glossy, four-color materials convey a finality of institutional purposes. They suggest that the purposes of the campaign or the programs featured within it have been fully formed and designed and only need the donor's money to flourish. Yet donors are far more likely to give to initiatives that they have a voice, if not a hand, in shaping.

Since a major gift decision unfolds over months and entails numerous interactions between prospective donors and institutional representatives, it is far wiser to create simple, but elegant materials— such as brief white papers and customized proposals—that invite and create the potential for incorporating reasonable feedback. You cannot market prospects into philanthropic submission, but you can help them to appreciate and support the agency of your institution with compelling, but simply presented, content.

Feature admirable people doing admirable things

People identify with people. While potential donors who lost a mother to cancer or a father to a heart attack might be motivated to ameliorate the impact of those diseases, they will be further motivated if they learn that researchers or doctors in those fields also lost parents to those diseases and then dedicated their lives to mitigating the diseases' impact. Programs that seek to ameliorate disease or promote economic growth or social justice are of immense importance, but donors are far more apt to give larger gifts when they are able to read about or meet faculty, students, and staff who are on a personal quest to make a difference and who can define how they hope to convert specific levels of investment to specific outcomes.

Substantive engagement (fewer frothy events) with donors

Attendance at campaign-launch events, campaign meetings, or celebrations must be curated over time through active listening, long-term relationship building, demonstrations of institutional accountability and integrity, and sustained substantive engagement. Institutions that have not done these things well cannot compensate for them by hosting flashy events, offering expensive meals, or staging activities in expensive or unusual locales. Such activities will only draw those who are currently giving and affiliated and will not induce them to give more than they might otherwise. Institutions that have built constituent depth and demonstrated agency and integrity don't need to engage in such activities. Campaign events should be designed to showcase specific content areas and to invite dialogue with those who have the most to contribute to them and who care most about advancing them.

Preserving and expanding the ranks of loyal donors

As noted previously, the people who are most likely to give the largest gifts in a campaign are not only those who have given previously, but also those who have given for a decade or more. Institutions that become overly consumed with achieving higher dollar goals each year pay too little attention to donor attrition. The loss of loyal donors, particularly those who have given for five years or more, constitutes a significant setback to the institution's long-term ability to secure major gifts and estate gifts.

The comprehensive campaign of the future should be based on the slow, but certain dynamics of philanthropy and place a far greater emphasis on donor retention and wooing back lapsed donors. Securing larger amounts from a few donors, a growing reality due in part to formation of wealth in recent decades, advances the short-term interests of an institution, rather than its long-term health. Responsible fiduciaries should strive to counter this trend.

Finally, a critical element in donor retention and donor recapture is avoiding over-asking, a chronic and pervasive disease found in many organizations. Asking for money too often, spending too much on impersonal forms of solicitation, doing little to outreach to donors beyond asking for more, confusing donors with too many giving options, and asking them to give to everything that comes down the pike. In the context of the comprehensive campaign, this may take the form of the double ask (continue to give to the annual fund plus make a gift to the campaign) or the triple ask (the previous two plus an estate gift). This approach emphasizes the vehicles or means of giving over what is to be accomplished by giving. It does little to understand or honor the donor's philosophy of giving.

Despite efforts to get donors to give in two or three ways, annual fund proceeds, during most comprehensive campaigns, decline. Many donors simply do not understand why they need to give to multiple funds or varying purposes. They assume a gift is a gift and will direct it to the area that the institution emphasizes. Constant requests can make donors feel inadequate or unappreciated and cause them to turn to organizations that offer greater psychic rewards, more tangible appreciation, and clear evidence of impact.

Recognition of more diverse student and alumni cohorts

The thousands of institutions that make up our system of higher education have become increasingly diverse as we search for more cost-effective ways of providing high-quality education to a wider swath of the population. In the face of constrained resources stemming from demographic challenges (fewer traditional college-age students) and greater competition, institutions will need to customize their approaches to local, historic, economic, and cultural realities. Just as a general or political strategist wouldn't run the same campaign in every place, comprehensive campaign strategists, including board members, must make sure their institutions don't fight the last war or somebody else's war.

Redefining Our Terms

The comprehensive campaign of the past grew out of distinguished institutions with long histories, hallowed traditions, strong followings, and deep pockets. The campaign of the future will grow out of and reflect a diversity of backgrounds and aspirations. So as institutions seek to design campaigns that adapt to these new realities, questions may emerge on campuses and in boardrooms, including the following:

KEY QUESTIONS

Is the term "comprehensive" still appropriate or is there a better term that conveys a more disciplined approach?

When would it be appropriate to think of a campaign as comprehensive?

Would it not strengthen our hand to think about the future of the institution in terms of specific building blocks and programmatic objectives more?

The word "comprehensive" still has great utility, but it would benefit from a clearer definition. A comprehensive campaign still has meaning and relevance if it describes an effort that:

- Is an outgrowth of a thorough strategic-planning effort, one that has taken objective stock of the institution's assets and weaknesses—including its ability to inspire alumni to take an active ownership stake—as well as the opportunities and threats those assets represent, and then has charted a unique and compelling course toward greater societal relevance;

- Reflects extended listening exercises and the hopes and concerns expressed by key constituents;

- Encompasses all key campus constituents—students, faculty, staff, alumni, parents—and calls them to higher levels of service;

- Is comprehensive in its outlook, including the segments of society and the range of societal purposes it seeks to serve; and

- Is far-reaching in the way it seeks to convert investment to lasting societal gain.

However, the term is all but outmoded if it aspires to gain as much as possible for a multiplicity of internal stakeholders, including lots of endowments and buildings, while offering broad platitudes about institutional excellence, but no specific promises of societal return on investment. Leaders of institutions who are content to let internal stakeholders pursue their self-interest with the assumption that it will serve the whole have no reason to engage in a campaign because no real institutional decision-making or direction-setting has occurred.

Leaders of institutions who are content to let internal stakeholders pursue their self-interest with the assumption that it will serve the whole have no reason to engage in a campaign because no real institutional decision-making or direction-setting has occurred.

In light of this, the one word that may give "comprehensive" a run for its money in defining the next wave of campaigns is "strategic." And what is most likely to define a truly strategic campaign is not the usual buckets and categories of giving, but proposals for a set of specific projects that, if sufficiently funded, promise to produce specific measurable outcomes.

Rather than ask donors to give to scholarships or financial aid, the project-based approach might define the characteristics of students most prized by that institution; the number of students with those characteristics currently enrolled; the number the institution thinks it could enroll in what period of time; and the level of investment required to recruit and retain them through graduation. Every featured project would have to answer these questions:

- Why is this important to the institution and the purposes it serves?

- Why are we in a particularly strong position to achieve these purposes?

- What is the state of this field, program, or service today?

- Where do we think it could be in two to five years?

- Why do we believe this goal is attainable?

- What will it cost to get there?

- What return will it yield to society and when?

- How we will measure success?

As sensible as this approach may sound to some, it is certain that it will not be met with universal glee within institutions. Mythologies persist in the minds of internal stakeholders, causing them to believe the proverbial there is "a lot of low-hanging fruit out there" or, perhaps stated more bluntly, "there are a lot of rich people who would give wads to us if they could only see how swell we are."

But consider that purpose-driven support of higher education has long been provided by various philanthropic foundations. The most significant of them have promulgated program guidelines (or areas in which they are willing to consider proposals for funding) and have required petitioners to define how funds would yield programmatic improvements. They have also required progress reports of institutions that received funds.

Philanthropic foundations typically do not impose goals or deliverables on their recipients so much as ask them to define how they would use the money and to what outcomes they would hold themselves accountable. The requesters of the funds make the promise, and the foundation holds them accountable to their word.

One of the new realities that colleges and universities must confront is the growing tendency of individual philanthropists, particularly those of significant means, to act like foundations. Increasing numbers of them define the areas that they are willing to fund and stipulate that the requesting entity say how the funds are to be used, what goals are to be reached, how progress will be monitored, and how they will keep the foundation informed. They are, in effect, asking for a stewardship plan as a condition of giving.

College and university leaders who find such conditions overly onerous need not request support from these individuals, but a confident institution would probably want to hold itself to high standards and strive toward specific outcomes. It is not only the right thing to do, but also the smart thing.

However, there is a more practical issue at play here. Even wealthy individuals who have a deep and abiding interest in your institution and are quite enthused about a particular initiative still will struggle with how much to give. The difference between receiving either $2 million or $5 million from that donor likely will not be determined by how fervently you ask for it or how well-written your proposal might be, but rather by how clearly you define the use and impact of the larger amount.

- Many elements of traditional comprehensive campaigns are ill suited or inappropriate to new and emerging philanthropic realities.

- The campaign of the future will need to place greater emphasis on content, agency, and societal return on investment; it will require institutions to heighten their focus on specific purposes and be able to demonstrate return on donors' investment.

- Accountability and impact projects will need to be built into institutional materials and made apparent to prospects at the outset of philanthropic discussions.

CHAPTER VI: MAKING EFFECTIVE USE OF CAMPAIGN COUNSEL

Most people and institutions have a tendency to hear what they want to hear and interpret data in a way that reinforces existing assumptions. Institutional leaders should therefore consider the use of campaign counsel to see if they are capable of providing the following benefits:

- A willingness to speak truth to the powers that be;

- The opportunity for prospects and key stake-holders to speak the truth through them, in confidence and with candor;

- Objective and comparative analyses of data, including assessment of the depth of constituent affiliation and strength of prospect and donor pipelines;

- Rigorous assessments of the efficacy and competitiveness of the case for support;

- Ways to improve prospect-engagement strategies;

- Objective evaluations of staff and internal capabilities;

- Campaign funding and staffing plans and projections; and

- Review and development of policies necessary to govern campaigns, including national standards for counting gifts, gift-acceptance policies, and prospect coordination and management.

While such expertise will allow institutions to learn from the successes and failures of other institutions, consultants are not omniscient, and boards need not treat their recommendations as unimpeachable. There are a lot of consultants to choose from, which means they are representative of the bell curve distribution of human talent—some very good, some very bad, and lot of average ones in between.

Once again, institutional leaders can help their institutions choose the right consultants by asking the right questions, both *about them* as they check references and *of* them in direct dialogue. The hallmarks of good consultants include the following:

- Extensive fundraising experience and significant success, particularly in vice president or chief advancement officer positions;

- Evidence of strategic planning and strategic-thinking skills, manifested in the ability to align institutional competencies with external funding opportunities or to detect lack of alignment between the institution's direction and the donors expected to support it;

- Strong analytical skills evident in the ability to know what data to look for, how to interpret those data, and how to use them to forge effective strategies;

- Ability to listen, but also to read between the lines and understand what people are really saying;

- A willingness to try to understand what makes each culture unique, including strengths and limiting factors, and to develop customized approaches that bring out the best in each client;

- A commitment to the institution and the mission it represents (not captive of any single interest or person within the campus); and

- Loyalty to clients, which might manifest itself in behaviors such as not selling services they don't need, protecting their interests by helping them minimize risks and avoid controversy, and keeping their confidences.

Consultants should be prepared to share the following information with institutions that are considering hiring them:

- The business model of their firm and how they determine what to charge clients;

- What differentiates their firm and when, where, and how they have brought innovations to the field;

- The standards they employ in determining who can work for their firm as a consultant;

- Specific value-added strategies that they and their firm brought to three different clients;

- How they customize their approaches and serve very different clients;

- Their greatest successes as a fundraiser and a fundraising leader and how they will transfer the lessons learned to your institution;

- Two or three cases in which they used data to help clients see opportunities or obstacles that the clients had not seen before;

- How they have used various feasibility studies to help clients understand how to strengthen their relationships with their most promising prospects or to retool their case for support so that it had greater donor appeal;

- What they have seen in your institution, either strengths or weaknesses, that they have not seen in other clients, and how they would recommend you leverage the former and mitigate the latter.

In helping their institutions find the right consultant—one who best complements the leadership skills of the president and vice president for advancement—institutional leaders should ask the following questions:

- Which individual in the firm will be our lead consultant and primary point of contact?

- How much time will he/she expect to devote to us?

- How many other clients will our consultant be serving at the same time?

Institutional leaders should also keep in mind the following:

- The consultant who best serves your purposes may be the least like you; in other words, hiring a consultant because he or she "fits in" or is popular with the staff may deprive your campaign of fresh eyes and a new perspective, may leave you in the same old ruts, and may blind you to new possibilities.

- The size of a firm is no guarantee of more or less service. A big firm with 25 consultants serving 175 institutions is not likely to provide your institution more or a wider range of services than a small firm of 5 consultants serving 25 institutions; the large firm offers a consultant to client ratio of 1:7 while the small one offers a ratio of 1:5.

- In a big firm, each consultant may operate from his or her own approach and philosophy, whereas in a small firm consultants may subscribe to a particular set of principles.

- If the institution pays a retainer for campaign counsel, make sure to define the work to be done over a period of time and the specific services to be provided.

- Your consultant, even when quite capable, may be no more skillful or accomplished than your best staff; overvaluing consultants at the expense of staff is a good way to drive your best staff into consulting.

What to Expect and Not Expect from a Consultant

If a consulting firm is selected, the vice president for advancement should be comfortable in giving the president direct access to that consultant to receive independent corroboration of the direction being set and to secure direct confidential advice on how he or she can be more effective as a fundraiser or as an campaign architect. By the same token, presidents have every right to be concerned if the relationship between the vice president and the consultant seems to be one of mutual self-protection or mutual aggrandizement. Further, the board should expect to engage with the lead consultant on a quarterly basis, or each time the board meets. Since a consultant is there to provide objectivity, the board should quiz him or her on what needs to be done, where the institution is and is not progressing, how it compares to others, and what it can learn from them. A confident president and vice president for advancement should be comfortable giving a board direct access to a consultant during board meetings to ask probing questions about the state of the campaign and the strategies employed, but board members should avoid engaging him or her in personnel matters such as individual performance evaluations, or the operational details of campaign or fundraising management, or the interpersonal relationship between the president and vice president of advancement. Board members should not expect access to confidential donor interviews or strategies used with individual donors.

Usually, the first task a campaign consultant is asked to take on is an objective assessment of the institution's readiness for a campaign. A board should ask for a broad institutional assessment, not just one dealing with tactical and operational abilities of the fundraising office. As the table below suggests, a successful campaign requires the commitment and coordination of many stakeholders and includes many functions. Fundraising is part of advancement (the totality of means employed to build constituency around the institution's mission), and advancement is part of carrying out larger institutional objectives.

FIGURE 4: FOUR PILLARS

Institutional Narrative	Articulators	Vehicles	Sources of Support
Purpose (Strategic Priorities)	Board	Events	Alumni
	President	Promotional Materials	Parents
Possibility (Measurable Impact of Implemented Priorities)	Academic Leaders	Rituals	Foundations
	Faculty	Website	Corporations
	Advancement	Publications	Independant Philanthropists
	Students		
	Staff		

This chart demonstrates the importance of an institution getting its story straight and making the story interesting, building commonalities of purpose within an institution, finding and deploying those who can best exemplify and/or articulate the story, and coordinating all vehicles of communication to tell the story and learn from the responses.

Case for Support

Using the institutional readiness chart as a road map, we can see the importance of the institutional narrative—the case for support: the story of the institution's highest purposes and greatest possibilities that can be told in a consistent, authentic, and compelling way by its principal articulators. It presents an opportunity for an institution to project agency as a means of engendering private support and to seize the opportunity to interest donors who have many choices for supporting important causes and issues.

The case cannot be a call for loyalty or a reliance on sentiment (for example, Ever Steadman); it must speak to specific differences to be made, why they are important, and why the institution is uniquely positioned, prepared, and poised to make them. A poorly prepared case statement, when previewed by an institution's most promising prospects, can deflate and discourage philanthropic interests. The best consultants, therefore, will do the following:

- Formulate a case for support that draws on a strategic plan with strong analytical foundations and/or significant and substantive input from the institution's best thinkers (including board members and alumni);

- Spot a weak case and what makes it so, and urge the institution to spend more time on planning, priority setting, and depiction of the institution's plan;

- Predict how major donors are apt to respond to elements of the case that may be out of sync with market realities, based on other recent work they have done;

- Disclose if they or their firm plan to interview an institution's top prospects on behalf of other clients without disclosing the other client(s) or anything gleaned from the interview(s) to avoid the appearance of any conflict of interest; and

- Caution an institution not to rush into a feasibility study or recommend that a weak case be previewed by a large number of prospective donors.

Institutional leaders need to have a grasp of the business models employed by various consulting firms and understand that the most lucrative portions of most contracts are in the assessment of an institution's readiness to undertake a campaign, and feasibility studies based on interviews with a large sample of the most likely potential donors. Therefore, institutional leaders must make sure that they are not acceding to recommendations made by consultants that are more about the profitability of the firm than the insight gleaned from the proposed interviews.

Relatively small samples of interviews with likely potential donors (15 to 30) can yield as much insight as large samples. And if sensitive issues begin to surface in feasibility studies, such as a widespread discontent with the case for support or a consistent lack of confidence being expressed in the leadership of the institution and/or advancement, ethical consultants will tell their clients immediately. This will allow the institution to regroup, rethink, and refine its case before proceeding with a larger sampling.

In some cases, a president, vice president for advancement, or consultant may argue for a large sample of prospects to make them feel a part of a campaign, to yield specific insights into individual donor passions, or to keep prospects from having their feelings hurt by being excluded from the study. Yet trustees and presidents need to weigh the costs in consultant time and travel against the outcomes.

Further, many significant prospects have been interviewed by many consultants representing many clients, and they have grown weary of what they see as nothing more than an effort to set them up as a prospect. Many, therefore, will rebuff the request for the feasibility-study interview.

When the results of a feasibility study are presented, the board should ask how many interview requests were made, how many people agreed to be interviewed, and how many declined. Since those chosen for feasibility studies are presumed to be the institution's very best prospects—the proverbial 10 percent who give 90 percent of the total—the rate of rejection from this carefully selected group will be an early indication of how realistic the advancement office has been and perhaps even of the viability of the campaign. Board members and presidents should prevent a weak case for support from being distributed too widely.

Good consultants are like good scouts. When coupled with strong leadership and sound planning, they can help lead an organization across the philanthropic terrain to a better place. They will be familiar enough with that terrain to know how to avoid slippery slopes. They will be data driven and able to ascertain which data points reveal the best path forward. They will know how to deliver critical information in a neutral manner and when to warn, reassure, or rally their clients at various stages of the journey.

Institutional leaders must understand the boundaries of consultancy. Even great scouts cannot make up for weak leaders. They cannot be the president's or chief fund-raiser's buddy, protecting one or two people at the cost of the whole enterprise. They can't serve as interim advancement leaders or occupy an office on campus. They have to maintain a certain distance. They have to know the terrain from years of deep experience, but they can't assure specific outcomes. They can only tell you the best road to follow under the current circumstances. And, if you want to cut to the heart of the matter, ask your consultant, "What's the best piece of advice that you have given us that we haven't followed as much as we should have?"

Institutions fortunate enough to have a president and/or vice president with previous campaign experience may have less need for ongoing external counsel provided by one firm over the course of the campaign, but may still benefit from occasional, more focused reviews from a variety of firms. For instance, an institution in a campaign may choose to secure consulting services from one firm or one consultant in that firm that specializes designing and pursuing mega-gift opportunities, and months later, from another firm with proven capability in increasing annual fund levels. In addition, institutional leaders would be wise to call upon other sitting or recently retired presidents and vice presidents for advancement who are leading or have led highly successful campaigns to secure "real time" knowledge about critical success factors.

KEY TAKEAWAYS

- Campaign consultants should be a source of expertise, comparative knowledge, and best practice, both current and emerging, in planning and executing campaigns. They should be willing to challenge inappropriate institutional orthodoxies and unsubstantiated approaches to campaign planning and execution.

- Consultants should be dedicated to working within institutions, finding organic strengths, assessing how they relate to external opportunities, and then proposing a customized plan for relating the former to the latter. They should not offer the same plan to a variety of institutions with varying missions and cultures.

- Institutional leaders should explore the consulting firm's business plan and incentives to make sure that consultants are not merely emphasizing services that have the greatest profit margins for their firms, but instead are responding to institutional needs and facilitating opportunities unique to each institution.

THE REAL UTILITY OF A CASE FOR SUPPORT

Institutional leaders should understand that the term "case" can be applied to different instruments at different institutions. They should stress the importance of defining what it means at their institution, how it is to be used, and how it can be constructed for maximum effectiveness. A case for support, when well conceived and constructed and appropriately employed, is a critical component in building a cohesive comprehensive campaign.

A case is a master document that is written initially as an internal preparation and training tool. It is the means by which a strategic plan is turned into an a broad philanthropic prospectus, which later will be used to generate multiple cases for specific purposes, as well as white papers for specific initiatives and proposals for specific donors. The creation of the master case for support ensures consistency, which is critical to the establishment and enhancement of institutional identity.

The master document should not only make a case for how private funds can be used to advance strategic purposes and leverage institutional agency, but should also show how private support can be used in conjunction with other sources of support and institutional decisions and disciplines to create and broaden margins of excellence.

It demonstrates that tuition dollars can only take the institution so far in responding to societal need, and that tuition should be raised as little and as infrequently as possible to ensure that students and their families receive the greatest value at the most reasonable cost and so that alumni can begin lives and careers with as little debt as possible. It also speaks to what the institution has done and will do to manage its collective resources, including reducing inefficiencies and redirecting resources from under-performing to high-performing parts of the institution to ensure that private support is pure leverage.

THE REAL UTILITY OF A CASE FOR SUPPORT, CONT.

Private donors want assurance that their contributions will add as much value as possible and will not be diluted to cover the basic needs of the institution or to perpetuate dysfunction. Being prepared to address these issues at the outset of a campaign and demonstrate efficiency and integrity anticipates and mitigates an issue of growing concern to donors and establishes an ongoing commitment to accountability throughout the campaign.

Once an institution has defined how private dollars will magnify strengths and build on other sources of support, it can then make a case for institutional agency with a clear, convincing articulation of the following:

- Greater societal issues or opportunities to be addressed;

- The institution's unique competencies to address them;

- Initiatives for which private funds can be converted most effectively to institutional and societal gain;

- The private support necessary for each initiative to realize its goals; and

- The private support necessary to strengthen core functions.

Without a powerful master case, fundraisers and institutional representatives make their own rationales for private support, and the institution speaks with a confusion of tongues. This malady, while not fatal, undercuts an institution's ability to mobilize constituents' energy around core purposes and to channel it into strategic initiatives that benefit the entire institution and facilitate its collective agency.

THE REAL UTILITY OF A CASE FOR SUPPORT, CONT.

In the early stages of a campaign, an evolving draft of a master case for support is a means of building a coalition of purpose, as well as confidence in and clarity about the institution's direction. It should circulate among those people on whom campaign success will depend, including:

- The president or chancellor's cabinet

- Deans and other key academic officers

- Senior faculty members/thought leaders

- Student leaders

- Key administrative leaders

- Alumni and parent councils

- Advisory boards

- The board of trustees

It would also be wise to use the evolving case as a means of engaging students in focus groups to help the institution understand and demonstrate respect toward those who will be asked to support the institution in the near future.

While this may seem like a laborious process, board members should remember that the more diligent an institution is in eliciting the advice and testimony of its internal and external stakeholders, the more genuinely it listens, and the more candidly it responds, the more it increases the likelihood of fundraising success. Eliciting stakeholder opinion, therefore, saves time and money and produces a far greater return and more enduring moral and financial support. A case that is viewed only as a sales tool will do little to engender or inspire support.

PART 2: ORGANIZATION AND EXECUTION

CHAPTER VII: FROM PLANNING TO IMPLEMENTATION: THE ROLE OF THE BOARD

With our conceptual building blocks in place, we can now turn to the role of the board at specific points and phases in the planning and implementation of a comprehensive campaign. Here we begin with the crucial juncture of shifting from the planning phase to the implementation phases.

The most strategic questions that a board can ask its president and senior administrative team as they seek to convert a strategic plan into a campaign plan include the following:

- Which of our strategic imperatives are the most and the least likely to attract private support? Which have the potential of drawing significant levels of new support? How do we know?

- How can we convert these initiatives into campaign projects so that private supporters can see that we are driving toward specific outcomes, by specific dates, and not just asking them to fund open-ended processes?

- Do we have a faculty or staff champion for each of our spotlighted initiatives? If not, why are we featuring it? Why are we asking donors to make a significant investment without giving them the opportunity to look into the eyes of the person charged with implementing it? Are we compromising ourselves, including the development staff, if we try to raise money for something that we are not ready to implement?

- Do we have a potential lead donor with a proven philanthropic record and a demonstrable passion for each spotlighted initiative or what it represents?

- Will our highlighted initiatives strengthen the core of the institution by creating a wider margin of excellence in our best programs, attracting or leveraging income from other sources (including increased student enrollments) or creating greater economies of scale?

- How many of these initiatives are truly cross-disciplinary and designed to bring about more sustainable internal collaboration and greater cost efficiencies?

- Are we seeking to replicate the efforts of other institutions or are we seeking ways to collaborate and create larger strategic alliances that will show philanthropists that our perspective and mission extends beyond the institution?

- Are we prepared to implement the spotlighted projects when pledges to them are fulfilled?

The more forethought an institution gives to these questions, the more it will enhance its ability to convert investment into strategic advances.

As strategic campaign agendas are formed, board members should be asking themselves some additional tough questions, including:

- Am I excited about where this is going?

- Will it be easy for me to get behind one or more of these initiatives? Would I be comfortable urging a close friend or relative to take a closer look or get involved with one of them?

- Do I see my values and purposes reflected in one or more of these initiatives or in the whole effort? Of all the organizations or causes I might give to, is this emerging as something that I will want to make my greatest philanthropic priority?

Board members will be among the first to be solicited in a campaign. The leader of the institution and the vice president of advancement will look to board members to give generously, whether that expectation has been stated or not. The logic behind their assumptions should be clear:

- If the people responsible for holding the institution in trust are not committed to enhancing its value, who is more apt to be interested?

- If those who have the most influence in shaping the direction of the institution are not enthused about where it is going, how can they expect people with less influence to be excited?

125

- If those who know the institution best are not its most ardent and visible advocates, how can they expect those who know it less well to be more enthusiastic?

- If those who selected the president and have the most substantive interactions with him or her aren't singing his or her praises and opening doors to other donors, how can they expect others to play these roles more effectively?

While no institution should feel entitled to a board member's giving regardless of how it performs, no board member should feel completely unobligated to give, no matter how well the institution performs.

If board members feel the agenda is weak, they have a fiduciary obligation to speak up, challenge it, and suggest ways in which the agenda could be made more strategic. Strategy is the means by which internal aspirations are honed to adapt to external realities, and no one is in a better position or has a greater obligation to bring those external realities to bear than the board itself.

Board members who see the need for an external reality check, but believe that they do not have sufficient knowledge or experience to provide it, should urge the administration to seek that perspective from others more qualified to provide it—a point we will develop further in the next section. Only a weak or inattentive board allows a weak strategic plan or feeble case for support to get past it.

In addition, since effective campaigns are predicated on rigorous strategic thinking and decision-making, the planning and execution of a campaign cannot be delegated to the board's advancement committee and rubber stamped by the larger body. While the advancement committee should have primary responsibility for the coordination of campaign efforts and serve as the primary interface with the advancement office, the entire board must see the creation and advancement of strategic direction as one of its most important functions.

When consultants are brought in to help revive faltering campaigns, the first place they should look is giving by board members. If it is well below the average (25 percent of the campaign total for four-year institutions), they should zero in on the level of board engagement, including in the strategic-planning process in the run-up to the campaign. In most instances, there is a powerful correlation between the time and effort a board gives to a task and the level of support members provide for it. Evidence of insufficient time and effort allocated to campaign planning and execution can be found in board minutes.

Therefore, as boards weigh the merits of investing in a campaign, they should also consider the time, talent, and resources they are willing and able to devote to it. In terms of time, the most precious commodity of all, boards should allocate the following time, above and beyond what they give to the development of a strategic plan:

- A full-day retreat to hammer out the campaign agenda, review policies governing it, and determine how success will be defined, how progress against long-term goals can be monitored quarterly, and how labor will be divided (with particular attention to the role of the board chair, president, and vice president for advancement);

- A willingness to commit at least four hours each month to fulfill the campaign task to which they have agreed (examples of which will be enumerated later);

- A half-day of training to gain a factual grounding in the dynamics of philanthropy and fundraising, the institution's current fundraising assets and potential liabilities, how board members can be most helpful in the campaign, a review of the essential tasks, and how to secure individual commitments to those tasks.

Board members who chafe at the concept of being trained or oriented for a campaign or resist it altogether may do so because they think they know what there is to know or simply find the subject matter uninteresting or unworthy of their time. Yet, the active participation of board members is a prime determinant of campaign success. Training is important for several reasons, including:

- Many board members are so long and deeply affiliated with their institutions that they may not realize the challenges in raising money from those less informed or interested.

- Many board members equate fundraising with glad-handing, a low-level function that can be delegated to amiable, lower-level personnel. Training can help board members understand that the actual "ask" is the least important part of the process and that the definition of purpose, the strategic alignment of interests, and structured, substantive engagement of discerning philanthropists requires great skill and brings great joy.

- Board members who are reticent or somewhat introverted assume that fundraising requires a kind of back-slapping extroversion, but it does not. Fundraising is best served by good listeners who know how to work patiently, but persistently to link donor interests to institutional purposes.

- No responsible board member can vote for a comprehensive campaign and then duck the responsibilities associated with it. Among the most important of those responsibilities is to testify to the institution's relevance and agency, in depth and detail.

- The few hours of intensive training at the outset, when prorated over the life of the campaign, constitute an extraordinarily modest investment in an effort that could, if supported by all, yield immense benefits.

As board members are encouraged to play larger roles in the campaign, they have every right to insist on training and staff support. Yet one of the ways board members can assist their institutions in keeping the cost of fundraising to reasonable levels and extend the reach of the president, academic leaders, and advancement staff is to require as little staffing and personal support as possible. This can be facilitated by a collective institutional commitment to record keeping and the creation of a repository of information from which all may draw and to which all should contribute.

Given that the average major gift unfolds over 21 months, entails nine interactions, and that a campaign seeks to create thousands of conversations around the potential of major gifts, board members should see the importance of building a storehouse of campaign-related material that will assist with substantive engagement of prospects. The repository should include the following:

- Strategic plans and related documents, including market research on the opinions and attitudes of key constituents;

- Key facts and figures about the university, including details about enrollment, curricular mix, budget, and educational philosophy;

- Lists of the institution's distinguishing features, honors and achievements, and rankings;

- Frequently asked questions (by alumni, parents and other key constituents) and the official answers to them;

- White papers describing critical initiatives and descriptions of major projects underway or planned in the next few years; and

- Recent successes and recently funded initiatives, including those with government contracts.

In the absence of such information, conversations break down and prospective donors lose interest or wonder about the lack of follow-up to meetings on initiatives that piqued their interests. Even worse, development staff and other institutional representatives, if inadequately trained or unarmed with institutional plans and position papers, will stress what they think is most important to fund, even if it is less fundamental to the strategic plan or they will entertain ideas from donors that are not strategic and represent projects that would obligate the institution to underwrite more than the donor gives.

Boards and presidents should come to realize that over-seeing a strategic campaign involves far more than just determining how much each fundraiser should be expected to raise each year, how many prospects each fundraiser should handle, and how many more fundraisers will be needed to reach the campaign's goals.

Indeed, as an institution imagines or plans in earnest for a campaign and contemplates a campaign budget, board members need to understand where resources should be invested in planning the campaign to improve their institution's fundraising in the short-term, medium-term, and long-term.

In the *short-term*, spending for analytics, market research, and other forms of field intelligence would help the institution understand the state of constituent relations overall, as well as where its greatest philanthropic potential lies. This would include determining the best categories of prospects (for example, long-term donors, former major gift donors whose pledges have been fulfilled, and donors who lapsed after giving for five or more years) and then the most promising individuals in those categories (for example, a loyal donor who has given significantly more in the past three years or a donor who has become a much more active and productive volunteer).

Investments that would pay off in the *medium-term* would include programs, strategies, and outreach initiatives that would engage more constituents more regularly and more productively in the life of the institution or in advancing a particular initiative. Board members, understanding that volunteers give 10 times more than non-engaged donors, should make sure their institutions are investing in this kind of strategic capacity-building.

Influencing fundraising over the *long-term* would be investments in offerings and services that would deepen student and alumni appreciation, strengthen constituent affiliation, and engage the institution's most impressive alumni where they work and live. One example of this would be developing an innovative internship program to create more interactions between like-minded students and alumni. This could also help ensure the relevance of the institution's curricular offerings.

> *Influencing fundraising over the long term would be investments in offerings and services that would deepen student and alumni appreciation, strengthen constituent affiliation, and engage the institution's most impressive alumni where they work and live.*

As board members participate in this stage of framing a campaign agenda and determining the budget, they should have ample opportunities to speak up and express their growing enthusiasm or concern. If board members haven't spoken up, the president and fundraising team should be able to assume that they are on board and are aware that they will be among the first solicited and are giving serious consideration to a leadership gift.

If board members are not prepared to make the campaign one of their top three philanthropic priorities or if board chairs are not prepared to make the campaign their top priority, they should consider relinquishing their positions before the campaign goes any further.

Key Takeaways

- As plans coalesce into a commitment to proceed with large-scale engagement of prospective donors, board members need to make sure that the institution is ready to implement the spotlighted initiatives as soon as first gifts are received and that those initiatives build on existing strengths and will be sustainable over time.

- Board members need to be thinking about their own commitments, including asking themselves which initiative of the campaign they can best participate in and be enthusiastic about. If there are none, they need to challenge the direction of the campaign or consider their involvement on the board.

- Board members should be willing to spend extra time in learning about campaign imperatives and training themselves to be effective advocates. They should not vote for a campaign if they are not willing to give additional time, talent, and treasure to the cause.

- As the institution moves toward implementation of the campaign, board members should make sure that short-term goals and strategies are nested within and complement medium-term and long-term strategies for building constituent strength.

CHAPTER VIII:
THE COMPREHENSIVE
CAMPAIGN IN PHASES

Let us contrast how the emerging comprehensive campaign might look compared to the traditional model and then explore how each phase will shape up.

Traditional	Emerging
Planning (largely internal)	Planning (adapting to external realities)
Establishing Objectives	Disciplined Priority Setting
Feasibility Study	Constituent Engagement
Quiet Phase (50 percent of total length of campaign)	Pilot Phase (Testing workability of concepts)
Public Stage	Proving Stage
Wrap-Up	Strategic Reassessment
Celebration	Refocusing Objectives

With this framework, let us look at the phases of the emerging campaign and explain why some of the distinctions above, though subtle, will allow board members to better steer their institutions toward the future.

Planning

As noted earlier, the traditional campaign tended to be based on planning exercises that were largely, if not exclusively, the result of internal deliberations, or synthesized compilations of the aspirations of faculty and staff as well academic and administrative leaders. They tended to be based on a significantly flawed assumption: We can continue to grow and do even more. For instance, if one was to review the strategic plans for major universities in the early 2000s, one would find a number of thorough and thoughtful plans, some of which were predicates for campaigns and others that were the results of new presidents wishing to take more careful and complete stock of their institution's present and future. However, this author has not been able to find a single instance of a plan developed in that period that even considered the potential of a significant economic down-turn. When the economy went into a precipitous fall in 2007, all the aforementioned plans were of little use in guiding their institution's future. By definition, a strategic plan should anticipate external threats and suggest the means of adapting to them.

The emerging campaign, therefore, must begin with one core assumption: Change will continue apace and we must remain alert to anything that could render us less relevant in the years ahead. While economic downturns and demographic shifts have had the most obvious impact on institutional aspirations in recent years and, by necessity, have been adapted to by most, other threats loom and will have an impact on campaigns of the future. Foremost among them, as noted earlier, is the growing disjuncture between institutions of higher learning and their alumni, who have been their greatest and most enduring sources of support. Therefore, the emerging campaign must not only be built upon a strategic plan that provides an honest accounting of the state of alumni relations, comparing pre-Boomers and Boomers to Millennials and post-Millennials, but the ensuing campaign should also be designed to keep a range of institutional representatives in active listening mode throughout the entire exercise and beyond.

Disciplined Priority Setting

Even if leaders of an institution have engaged in rigorous soul-searching during strategic planning, they will still be subject to stakeholder pressures, which may make it difficult for the president and his or her administrative team to focus the efforts of the campaign on a few areas in which internal competencies can be leveraged to greater societal service.

THE ROLE OF THE BOARD IN PRIORITY SETTING

A board can be helpful to the institution and its president by being willing to "play the heavy" and insisting on a broad institutional focus in its public sessions so as to make clear that the goal of the campaign is not "something for everyone." To further this, the board should communicate the following:

- The campaign seeks support to reach milestones in pursuit of specific strategic missions, not to fill the general coffers (and then distribute funds equally) or to reward specific disciplines or academic structures.

THE ROLE OF THE BOARD IN PRIORITY SETTING

- Philanthropists will expect tuition revenue to cover the basic needs of the institution and will expect the campaign to focus on the institution's aspirations to better serve social purposes.

- Money in support of campaign objectives will come in over time, including in five-year pledges that can be made at any point in the campaign (which means pledge payments in a seven-year campaign would be spread over 12 years) and deferred gifts that may be realized a decade or more after the campaign concludes. Therefore, reaching the campaign total does not mean that amount will be on hand at the end of the campaign or available for anything other than the designated purposes.

- People give for purposes; they choose the way to support those purposes given their age, values, and wealth. So the best way to secure endowment gifts is not to stress the need or desire for endowment, but rather the purposes that could be perpetuated by greater resources.

- Reaching strategic milestones and emphasizing societal service over institutional status will increase the stature of the institution, which in turn will enhance its ability to deepen constituent strength and to secure greater moral and financial support.

In short, the board must help the president establish and hold the fort regarding the pursuit of a few strategic priorities over the life of the campaign.

Capital Improvements

One changing reality that institutions must be attentive to is the increasing difficulty of raising money for capital improvements, particularly building projects of $20 million or more. The reason that we no longer use the term "capital campaigns" is the same reason that institutions need a strong reality check before moving out of the campaign planning phase: Many institutions have had to underwrite and/or incur debt because of overly ambitious building projects.

Noted throughout this book is the tendency to listen to the institution's most promising prospects (perhaps 20 to 100 people), which can present a skewed picture of donors' receptivity to capital improvements. Long-engaged donors of very significant means, for instance, may be very receptive to, and encouraging of, the building of expensive new structures. They may be prepared to provide lead gifts in the tens of millions of dollars, which might represent almost half of the cost. The prospect of an immediate, large gift may cause institutions to assume that the remainder of the project's cost will be relatively easy to secure. Recent history, especially recent years featuring dramatic recessions, tells us not to make that assumption. The reasons for declining interest in capital improvements are many and include the following:

- Very large gifts are required to build very large and expensive buildings. Those who cannot provide gifts of $250,000 or more may feel their gifts would be dwarfed by the major gifts to the project.

- Many donors, whether they have $50 million or $500,000 to give, believe they will have far greater impact by giving to people and programs and that endowments in those areas, whether for endowed chairs or scholarships, will live in perpetuity, while few buildings are likely to last for more than 50 years. Moreover, female philanthropists, who live longer and dispose of more wealth tend not to make large capital gifts, favoring people and programs over facilities.

- Entrepreneurial donors look askance at sinking a lot of money into fixed structures, sometimes because they believe the world may change so dramatically in the years ahead that the space will become obsolete in a decade or less. Others simply feel it is wiser to invest in people and programs that promote innovation.

- Many alumni, watching their alma mater go through an extended building boom where a construction crane somewhere on campus was a constant for two decades, have concluded that "they don't really need the money." They assume that an institution that can repeatedly attract major gifts in the tens of millions no longer needs support from donors of more modest means.

Given these and other factors, it is probably unwise for institutions to do the following:

- Allocate more than 15 percent of their campaign goal to capital improvements unless they are prepared to cover the gap between building costs and dollars raised by incurring new debt, using unrestricted or reserve funds, or scaling back building plans based on the money actually raised.

- Proceed with fundraising for a building project or projects without securing at least one-third of the total in a single lead gift (while recognizing that most institutions struggle mightily to raise the last 20 percent of building costs, especially the last five percent).

- Give the green light to a capital project without a well-developed, realistic prospect list that ident-ifies all possible sources of support, perhaps through a comprehensive feasibility study.

- Break ground without all costs covered (either through fundraising, rescaling, or augmentation with other funds or bonds).

- Leave a languishing building project on the fundraising market too long; if a capital project cannot be funded in 24 to 30 months, the initiative is likely dead in the water. Flogging the fundraising staff members to throw more effort at the initiative after that amount of time can only come at the expense of other more viable fundraising opportunities, if not the entire campaign.

The very worst scenario is to break ground with little or no money down on the building, and then task fundraisers to find donors who will backfill institutional debt. This is an invitation to an unmitigated disaster. Board members must make sure that money and effort are not put into a relatively hopeless cause while more hopeful initiatives, for which dollars would be easier to raise, sputter or fail for lack of effort. After all, I know of no one who has studied higher-education philanthropy who has reported that students, alumni, or alumni donors cited the most valuable and lasting impact of their education as "the facilities."

Constituent Engagement

Constituent engagement is the most critical component of campaign success. Because constituent strength, particularly alumni affiliation and engagement, has such a direct bearing on fundraising success in the short-term and long-term, significant time and effort should be devoted to engaging constituents in conceptualizing and crystallizing the purposes of the campaign.

In an ideal world, an institution's strategic fundraising plan would be built on recent and ongoing interactions with key constituents, but even if that is not the case, institutions can still establish these relationships before the campaign objectives are finalized. While the traditional campaign featured a feasibility study focused on the likely 10 percent of donors who will give up to 90 percent of the campaign goal, the emerging campaign takes into account the new realities. Its premise is that those capable of the highest level of giving are not seduced into that remarkable level by a charismatic fundraiser, but rather are developed over a decade or more through close and substantive affiliation. Thus, by listening to and responding to younger constituents who give more modestly, we can create the prospect pipeline of the future and benefit from their time and talent.

Constituent engagement, at its best, provides value to the institution in the form of advice, expertise, and candid feedback and benefits the individual by making him or her feel valued by the institution—and not just as a source of dollars. Effective constituent engagement in the context of a comprehensive campaign would seek constituents' early involvement in the framing and shaping of the institution's strategic directions.

How can an institution improve its ability to serve the students of the present and future without learning from its alumni? How can it ensure the relevance of its curriculum if it does not listen to alumni in emerging fields of learning, innovation, and international affairs?

The following scenarios will show board members the best and worst ways of increasing an institution's potential to secure the support of its alumni.

Scenario A

Institution A, with an annual alumni giving rate of 9 percent, creates a strategic-planning committee composed of faculty and staff members. After a year, the committee produces a strategic plan that calls for changing the conditions that prevent faculty members from doing their best work; building a more civil and collaborative campus community, while increasing the diversity of the faculty, students, and staff; extending the institution's global reach and opportunities for international exchange; and securing the resources necessary to achieve these goals.

The president embraces the committee's findings and, with a few tweaks here and there, directs the chief advancement officer to develop a campaign plan in support of them. The advancement chief directs his communications staff to develop campaign collateral materials that will dazzle prospects and tells his associate vice president of development to come up with a pyramid of prospects and sends the gift officers, armed with said dazzling material, to go in pursuit of those prospects while he and the president focus on selected "principal" potential donors. When alumni and other constituents are presented with the four- color campaign brochures, it is the first time they have heard of the strategic plan and the first time they have heard from their alma mater in a long time.

Scenario B

Institution B, whose alumni participation rate has dropped from 20 percent to 17 percent in the past two years, does the same thing as Institution A, but the president and vice president decide that it would be a good idea to preview the first draft of the strategic plan with alumni and other key constituents via a tour of the eight cities in which most of them live. Many loyalists, including current donors and already active alumni, attend and express tepid support, notwithstanding a few opinionated folks who say the new initiatives aren't very interesting and the somewhat-interesting ones aren't very new. The institutional representatives say they appreciate the candor but then proceed to convert the strategic plan into a case for support.

Scenario C

Institution C, which has been holding alumni participation at 29 percent for the past three years, has a new, active president who seeks out the opinions of her alumni and other key constituents in her frequent personal interactions with them. As she does, she begins to sense that alumni, prior to her arrival, have been disappointed by a lack of communication and that this has begun to erode affiliation, which she knows is an early indicator of future loss of support. Her background in business has left her with an appreciation of market research, so she insists on a

"Pulse of Alumni" survey in which generations of graduates are asked which aspects of the institution must continue in the face of change and which must change if the institution is to endure, adapt, and thrive.

When the results of that survey come in, she sees a disparity between the views that faculty and staff members hold of their performance and stature and the opinions and attitudes of alumni, particularly alumni who graduated in the past two decades. While some of those in her inner circle advocate a "branding" campaign to close the gap between the reality of their strengths and the perceptions of alumni, the president knows that perception is reality, both in terms of the accuracy of some of the assessments and the immutability of some opinions.

She asks her advancement operation to organize a national "listening tour" on her behalf and commits to visiting 10 cities where her university has the largest concentration of alumni and parents. As she conducts the tour, she hears many of the same issues that arose in the "Pulse of Alumni" survey, but with greater granularity and intensity of emotion. She realizes that she has inherited a significant and growing disjuncture between institutional perceptions and aspirations and alumni views and expectations and, more importantly, between what the university has been communicating and what most alumni have been hoping to hear, including real issues and real struggles. As the tour concludes, she realizes that the university must construct and implement an analytically driven, yet sensitive strategic plan to keep the gaps from widening.

She frames the exercise in such a way that alumni opinions and attitudes must be addressed as the most important part of the "opportunities and threats" portion, and then creates a steering committee to construct campus dialogues that address ways of turning negative alumni opinions, including those about poor communication, or not being afforded a voice in the institution's direction setting, into gateways to greater affiliation by building on the most positive aspects of alumni appreciation. Further, she stipulates that diverse alumni of various decades must make up 40 percent of the steering committee and that all drafts and iterations of the plan must undergo alumni review.

Alumni participation on the steering committee keeps the study process from turning completely inward. As a result, when drafts are vetted by alumni—including those who participated in the "Pulse of Alumni" survey, those who turned out for the president's listening tour, and other recently active alumni—they see that their voices have made a difference, that indeed the president and her team have heard them. More alumni begin to conclude that they matter to this president.

The president builds on this growing goodwill in open letters to alumni, sharing what she has learned. She asks her advancement officers to establish an "Alumni Town Hall" tab on the website so alumni can review the issues being discussed, see a tabulation of alumni responses to major strategic issues, and weigh in by adding their views to the evolving discussion.

As the strategic plan crystalizes, the president and her senior team begin imagining a campaign that will seek to secure support for the strengths that alumni believe are essential to preserve the institution while eliminating weaknesses they believe are damaging its stature.

Analysis of These Scenarios

While institutions A and B are rather flimsy straw men, and institution C is a bit of an ideal, the stark juxtaposition makes the central point: People will allocate their greatest support to that which they helped shape and in which they see themselves, their experiences, and their values represented. In short, there is a powerful correlation between "we the people" in planning discussions and "the more perfect union" proposals they support.

Philanthropy is often a means by which one generation seeks to transfer values and life's most valuable lessons to the next. Excluding alumni from the design of the curriculum and campus life works against the formation of an intergenerational compact—the desire of one generation of alumni to help those who followed them because they were helped in such significant ways by those who preceded them.

Philanthropy is often a means by which one generation seeks to transfer values and life's most valuable lessons to the next.

Reciprocity is the important philanthropic principle here. Alumni who feel the lack of it (for example, "My alma mater does little to reach out to me besides asking for money") rebuff requests from fundraisers and, increaseingly, any outreach from their alma mater, because they see it as subterfuge.

One obvious way an institution can create greater reciprocity with its alumni is by bragging less about itself and praising alumni more, when the praise is warranted, for being emblematic of the institution and living out its values through such means as alumni community service.

Community service, after all, is a critical consideration or sometimes a prerequisite in many admissions policies and is often a means by which applicants gain a competitive advantage. As a result, the volume of student service activity has increased in recent decades, often beginning in junior high school. Many students don't stop once they are admitted to college; they continue to be highly engaged in community service throughout their higher education and beyond. A study conducted in 2009 by VolunteerWorks and the Fidelity Gift Fund noted that those with the most years of higher education were the most likely to serve as volunteers throughout their lives.

Institutional leaders, particularly in light of the general decline of alumni support, must understand the need for and encourage this kind of reciprocal constituent engagement. They must also question, if not discourage, over-investment in the production of materials, events, and other activities for the sole purpose of fundraising. The repetition of fundraising appeals typically drives down constituent participation, which results in lower levels of contribution. When reviewing campaign budgets, discussed in more detail in Chapter IX, trustees should look for a balance between constituent-engagement activities (particularly those tied to fundraising) and events and communications that afford constituents some value without being overtly tied to fundraising.

Pilot Phase

The traditional comprehensive campaign features a period generally referred to as the "quiet phase" in which the institution's fundraising team seeks to secure leadership gifts from the best prospects, including the members of its board. If those donors yield something close to 50 percent of the campaign total in a reasonable period of time—generally two years—the campaign will "go public" and seek to secure the remainder of the campaign goal, if not more, from a wider swath of prospects who generally are less connected to the institution and less capable of making the largest gifts.

In this way, an institution can test the feasibility of the larger goal by seeing if its "choir" and most dedicated "congregants" will come up with half. If they come up with more, the goal will be increased; if they take a long time to get to half of the goal, the quiet phase can be extended until half the total is secured, thereby all but guaranteeing that the campaign will reach its projected total. An important part of the quiet phase is the feasibility study, discussed above, which generally entails an independent consultant requesting a confidential one-on-one interview with the institution's most promising prospects to explore how much they might give to the campaign and to discover anything that might serve as a barrier to or help encourage their optimal giving level.

Eliciting opinions in advance serves many important purposes, including:

- Testing whether internal aspirations do indeed align with external realities;

- Showing consideration and respect to one's major supporters by affording them a voice and responding to it, thereby increasing the likelihood of their giving generously;

- Picking up on concerns, frustrations, or hurt feelings that may be lurking among the most promising donors and thereby having the opportunity to mitigate them; and

- Affording the institution the opportunity to go back to the drawing board, if necessary, and reframe the campaign agenda or case so that it will have wider philanthropic appeal.

Though this technique has proven its value in the planning and execution of many campaigns, it has rarely been used to full effect or applied as broadly as it should be. For instance, some institutions fail to construct a truly "forensic" interview template for the feasibility study's interviews and come away with little more insight into the motivations of their top donors than when they began. Most studies focus only on their most wealthy donors, even those with low philanthropic propensity, and miss the opportunity to engage those who may be less conspicuous, but capable of giving generously. And many institutions limit the scope of their efforts to 100 or fewer prospects, a sample that may constitute those who are apt to give the largest gifts, but may not represent the interests and concerns of the larger constituent base.

Listening too closely to a narrow segment of constituents, no matter how much money they might represent, may cause an institution to lose touch with the majority of constituents and to launch a campaign that, once again, may boast "dollars up" at the cost of "donors down"—a worrisome long-term phenomenon.

In fact, sometimes a comprehensive campaign winds up imposing future costs on the institution. Very wealthy donors, for instance, may urge an institution to be aggressive in upgrading residence halls or athletic facilities, while dismissing the costs that may be passed on to students for maintaining them. Many alumni and other potential donors, however, may be very concerned about anything that would drive up cost, especially if it does not add value to the degrees offered or strengthen the employability of graduates.

The point is that board members should not think about the initial stage of a campaign as a "quiet phase," but rather as a "testing phase." They should encourage their administrative leaders to test appreciation, affiliation, and receptivity to key concepts and spotlighted initiatives across constituents (for example, alumni, parents, friends) and across segments of constituents (for example, age, gender, geography). If the results are positive, this indicates that there is sufficient reciprocity to proceed. If negative, in whole or in part, it would be far wiser to ease off the fundraising pedal and figure out through more active listening what constituents might be more interested in supporting.

THE ROLE OF THE BOARD IN THE PILOT PHASE

Board members can and should play many constructive roles in the pilot phase of the campaign, including the following:

Gathering Intelligence

A successful philanthropic campaign, just like a military or political one, is achieved by the acquisition and implementation of field intelligence. A skilled campaign consultant can be effective in creating a more intelligent and intelligence-driven campaign, but hiring one is certainly not the only way to go. Other skilled practitioners, including sitting presidents and vice presidents for advancement who are further along in their campaigns or who have recently concluded one, could bring invaluable testimony to board meetings. Board members could gather important intelligence and strengthen key donor relations by:

- Agreeing to serve as a relationship manager for two to five major donors to the institution,

THE ROLE OF THE BOARD IN THE PILOT PHASE

which would entail calling or visiting them over the course of a year to see if they feel their investment in the institution has been put to good use, if the impact of their gift has been communicated to them, and if there is more information (annual reports, budgets, lists of specific achievements) that would be helpful to them. When board members pay attention to high-level donors, it increases the likelihood of those donors giving again, more generously, and singing the praises of the institution in their spheres of influence.

- Interviewing friends and colleagues who have given to other institutions about their most and least satisfying giving experiences and sharing that information at board meetings so that institutional leaders can learn from good and bad practices.

- Attending a professional-development seminar (a growing number of them are tailored to training boards and board members) on their own or, when appropriate, with a member of the advancement team or a member of a larger delegation from the institution. The more that key players come to see the issues in an informed way, the more an institution can function as a team, rather than lapsing into finding fault with one another, as we saw in the Steadman example.

- Being visible as a representative of the institution at other civic events and in community organizations so that the institution is seen as a good citizen and so that board members can keep the administration apprised of the institution's actual standing in the community.

- Helping the institution forge alliances, whether through internships for students or linking institutional research to specific business and community interests.

Being Actively Engaged

Indeed, a board can have a great impact on a campaign by engaging in the activities noted above. A comprehensive campaign built on current and future agency of an institution allows various board members with varying personalities to contribute in a variety of ways. Few people like to raise or give money, but many people get excited about causes and purposes and, when they do, become natural advocates and eager donors.

One of the best indicators of a poorly conceived campaign is nominal board engagement, manifested by minimal and obligatory giving, with all aspects of fundraising (not just the asking) being done by the professional staff. On the other hand, one of the best indicators of a well-conceived campaign is high board engagement, manifested in individual board members engaged in specific agency-oriented initiatives, with board members spreading the word within their spheres of influence quite enthuse-iastically and giving so enthusiastically that it encourages others.

A powerful subtext in every successful campaign is institutional momentum, an increasingly widespread feeling that the institution is on the move, gaining relevance and distinction, and arousing, building, and deepening constituency. But a campaign that proceeds beyond the pilot phase without strong evidence of board enthusiasm and board generosity will limp the rest of the way.

Proving Stage

As new realities and an increased emphasis on agency make the "quiet phase" of a campaign increasingly inapt, the same is true of the "public phase" or "going public." If the initial phase of the campaign involves testing concepts, programs, and initiatives that demonstrate institutional agency and seeking initial funding from large investors, it seems logical to think of the ensuing phase as the "proving stage."

In this stage, the institution would seek to demonstrate the higher levels of agency made possible in the pilot phase and suggest how it could be extended even further through larger levels of funding. For instance, imagine an institution that, as a result of its strategic planning, defines service learning as one of its most defining and distinguishing features. It does so because of the following:

- It was among the pioneers of the service-learning movement (demonstrating a core institutional competency);

- Enrollment increased over time because of its appeal to students (showing sustained market appeal);

- Faculty members increasingly integrated it into their courses (cultural acceptance);

- A center for service learning was formed and funded through private contributions (community and philanthropic buy-in);

- Students logged so many hours in community service that the institution became a national leader in the number of hours logged per student per semester (cultural ingraining);

- Demand from community-based organizations increased so rapidly that the center's director and senior university officials found themselves in such a reactive mode that they began to lose sight of original purpose such that the model became less and less about benefitting students, faculty, and community (strategic resonance and reciprocity).

As a result of this strategic reconsideration, a new service-learning prototype was formed that incorporated elements of past success and projected new possibilities, including a wider service area, services that better corresponded to curricular offerings and nonprofit growth in the community and greater engagement of alumni.

This initiative became one of the five featured in the initial campaign plan, and it was met with a positive response by major donors during the testing period. Indeed, the former chair of the board, who had stepped down a year earlier, declared it was the most attractive project in the draft case for support and made an outright gift of $2.5 million to the initiative.

With that strong endorsement, the institution saw the opportunity to take the concept to a wider circle of prospects with the hopes of securing another $7.5 million. With $2.5 million in hand, the institution was able to project which of the featured objectives and milestones in this initiative could be reached in the next two years and which would require the receipt of additional pledges.

The president, after reflecting on the remarkable service of current and previous students, also saw an opportunity to build community and strengthen reciprocity. Therefore, as his university moved from the pilot phase (formerly the quiet phase), into the proving stage (formerly the public phase), he called upon all faculty, staff, and alumni to make a five-year pledge to personally engage in community service, in the name of the campaign. The service could be to the institution or cause of their choice: community, church, educational institution, and, yes, their alma mater. He said that every hour of every service pledge fulfilled was as valuable as every dollar donated and, therefore, the institution would be running two tallies—volunteer hours and dollars—and celebrating both. The total of the two, he said, would provide vivid testimony about the dramatic and lasting impact of giving through, not just to, the institution.

This vignette should allow institutional leaders to see that what causes a campaign to gather and accelerate momentum is not the campaign totals, the most remarkable gifts received, or the inspiring example of those who gave them. It is the demonstration of agency, the conversion of dollars into differences made. And as important differences are made and their positive forces are set in motion and multiply, enthusiasm and belief in the institution's greater agency grows.

THE ROLE OF THE BOARD IN THE PROVING STAGE

As agency is converted into impact, board members have a golden opportunity to engage those in their sphere of influence by asking them to see what has already been achieved and to lend their time and talent to see how it could be leveraged further. This is a great philanthropic moment—the opportunity to propel a proven product or service from good to great.

THE ROLE OF THE BOARD IN THE PROVING STAGE

Legitimate leverage excites the interests of significant philanthropists. Too few institutions understand the importance of leverage or think of it only in terms of a "challenge grant"— when a donor makes a gift of, say $1 million, on the condition that it be matched 1:1 by other donors. This appeals to many donors because no one wants to squander $1 million, and because they give in such a way that leverages their investment, they are able to get more value (for the institution and the purposes it serves) for their philanthropic buck.

However, leverage can also be achieved by leveraging government grants with philanthropy or vice versa. In addition, there are many public-private partnerships that can be further leveraged by philanthropy and through which philanthropists can achieve tremendous leverage on their investment. For instance:

- A university's advanced telecommunications and information-technology center receives a major grant from the state and sets to work leveraging it with business and industry in those fields in the form of sponsorships, equipment grants, internships, research collaborations, and philanthropic support.

- A university professor in urban ecology receives a large federal grant to develop "education stations" along the city's main river. This provides an opportunity for the advancement staff to engage prospects who appear to have converging interests—including those with a passion for environmental issues, science education, and inner-city education. The university's president seizes the opportunity to build a coalition with other civic organizations and school systems to ensure the maximum impact of the grant and to stimulate further urban development. Together these efforts lead to a grant from a major philanthropic foundation that is more than twice the amount of the professor's federal grant.

- A college that has been struggling to raise enough money for a performing-arts center goes back to the drawing board and reimagines the project as a multi-dimensional cultural center that would be erected on the periphery of campus so that it could serve as a physical and cultural bridge to the community. It develops a case that demonstrates how the facilities will be shared by multiple arts and educational organizations and how their students will commit themselves to community service in the area, including music students giving after-school lessons to K–12 students.

- A new design element—a piazza extending from the center into a subway station—would incorporate a vibrant array of small restaurants, studios, arts centers, and open-air concerts. This captures the imagination of a local, previously non-aligned philanthropist. Her gift, larger than the initial lead gift, allows the college to leverage the re-imagined larger and more vital concept to secure the support of business and industry and build a coalition of well-established philanthropists who see it as an opportunity to trigger greater cultural and economic development. This in turn is expected to attract more college-age students to the area.Interviewing friends and colleagues who have given to other institutions about their most and least satisfying giving experiences and sharing that information at board meetings so that institutional leaders can learn from good and bad practices.

The Role of the Board in the Proving Stage

In the various scenarios presented above, board members should see new realities and new opportunities, which they could use to enhance the offerings of their institutions aligned with important strategic purposes. Their skills and stature in the community or the state can be of immense importance in doing this. The most significant of these new realities is the advent of more discerning, exacting donors, which, in the main, is a positive development. Such donors cause institutions to think more carefully about the promises they make to individual donors and to demonstrate the impact of private gifts with greater precision. This, in turn, makes institutions more strategic and efficient. Support from these new donors, many of whom give quite generously, can take different forms, depending on their sensibilities, as shown in the following scenarios:

- Donors who act like foundations. Whether or not they form a family foundation, these donors define the causes or purposes to which they are willing to give. They respond only to those who approach them in the right way with the right initiative, screen out all others, and give only to those whose funding requests include budgets, project timelines, and projected outcomes.

- Donors who act like venture capitalists. They look for early-stage ventures that seek to achieve great things and have the potential to become self-sustaining. They become engaged early, contribute expertise, help shape the project, and see it through to completion.

- Donors recruited by the institution for a specific but exceptional ability that corresponds to an institutional need or opportunity. Based on this need, an initiative is formed to which the donor contributes considerable time and talent before committing treasure.

THE ROLE OF THE BOARD IN THE PROVING STAGE

There are, of course, variations on these themes with various donors having aspects of each type, but the trend is clear. Not only are the largest donors more likely to designate the specific use of their gifts, they are more likely to act like "philanthropic Missourians" who ask those requesting the funds to "show me" how they will be used, for whose benefit, and how the impact of the investment will be measured and assessed.

Such discerning donors, particularly if they have not given to an institution before, will rebuff approaches from advancement staff, even those with the most senior titles. Presidents, deans, and others may have more success, but only if they know the proclivities of these donors and approach them correctly. In other words, a president who seeks to connect with them to advance his particular agenda will not get far. He or she must demonstrate in advance or at a first meeting, that he or she knows who the potential donors are, what they care about, and is visiting them to explore an alignment of purposes. In some cases, presidents will not be able to secure the appointments without a referral from a trusted source; that is an area in which board members can have an impact by using their influence and stature to open the doors to discerning philanthropists.

Board members can also be of immense value in helping the institution understand the minds of venture philanthropists and prepare accordingly by doing the following:

- Being bold and forward-thinking in their plans and avoiding describing initiatives in terms of needs and processes (for example, green, global, and interdisciplinary studies);

- Defining a value proposition unique to the institution and showing how it can be leveraged to correspond to current or emerging realities;

THE ROLE OF THE BOARD IN THE PROVING STAGE

- Developing financials and budgets that demonstrate with some specificity the resources currently available and the investment increments that will be required to achieve specific performance outcomes; and

- Describing how initial investments can be converted into a sustainable enterprise, including how the initiative will generate revenue or attract investment from other resources.

These skills are not readily available to institutions of higher learning; while many institutions are full of remarkable and diverse talents, few have conceived, launched, raised capital for, or sustained a business enterprise, including the most accomplished business professors. Board members who have done those things can be exceedingly helpful in a variety of ways, such as:

- Helping leaders of specific initiatives understand the mindset of the entrepreneurial philanthropist;

- Preparing initiative leaders, through personal help and advice, to compete for funds by showing them the essentials of a business plan; and

- Helping academic administrators understand the mind of the philanthropic investor and the power of projecting institutional and/or societal return on investment, as well as on demonstrating exactly where certain levels of investment have the probability of producing the strongest results.

Yes, there will be those, including many presidents, who say to board members who press them on these points:

The Role of the Board in the Proving Stage

Wait a minute—this isn't philanthropy. There are too many expectations attached. This sounds much more like a contract.

We need flexible funds that I can use for broader purposes!

Board members can point out that donors of significant means are bombarded with broad requests and that people typically give based on personal value systems and the desire to have an impact on issues about which they care deeply. Further, many generous donors who have given to many institutions have begun to question if and how they have made a significant difference. But perhaps the best way to help internal stakeholders understand this situation is by stating the following:

- No one has to give us money.

- If we choose to seek their support, we must attempt to align our interests with those of donors. If we cannot, we should walk away from the negotiations.

- Most donors are not seeking to impose conditions on us, but are asking institutions of higher learning to bring them plans and projections that demonstrate with greater precision how private investment can have the greatest impact. If those plans and projections are lacking, donors will stipulate their own conditions.

- Managing and leveraging all resources for the greatest possible return can only make for a better institution and enhance its reputation.

Board members who are willing to represent external realities will have the most positive impact on shaping internal aspirations in such a way that their probability of success will be far greater.

Strategic Reassessment

As a traditional comprehensive campaign nears its goal or its final year, a significant effort is put into preparing to share the success through celebrations in order to thank and to recognize those who helped the institution reach its goal. The trouble with this approach is that it causes just about everyone to conclude that the goal has been met, that the institution has achieved its purposes, and that it will now go about putting all the money it has raised to good use. In such instances, constituents have a right to conclude that the institution won't need much more money anytime soon.

In such instances, constituents have a right to conclude that the institution won't need much more money anytime soon.

By shifting the emphasis away from broad or categorical goals to initiative-specific ones, and away from dollars raised to mission milestones reached, the emerging comprehensive campaign puts an institution not in the position of preparing to declare victory, but rather to conduct an open and thoughtful assessment about what has been done and what remains to be done. Rather than declaring an end to something, the emerging comprehensive campaign accounts for what it has achieved, what can be sustained, and what new adjustments need to be made, not for more money to serve more institutional purposes, but to better serve the larger purposes of community and society.

Because an institution's mission is a constant while the needs of society are ever-changing, broad goals such as the alleviation of suffering or helping more individuals realize their full human potential will remain worthy, but elusive; there will always be more work to be done.

Celebration and the sharing of success should be a key feature of today's campaigns, but celebrations for purposes achieved with dollars raised should be only incidental. As the initiatives featured at the outset of the campaign secure most of the investments required, greater emphasis should be on setting a new set of objectives that can and should be pursued. In this sense, the traditional campaign can be seen more like a political campaign or a military campaign; we know when they come to an end and the victors celebrate. The emerging campaign will project purposes to be served well into the future.

Refocusing Objectives

Carrying forward the logic established in the strategic-reassessment phase, the emerging campaign doesn't conclude with a formal celebration and cessation of effort, but with a recalibration of progress and a rededication to the next most-strategic goals, given current and changing realities. This model, when contrasted with the traditional comprehensive campaign, avoids donor fatigue because donors only become fatigued when they are asked for more than they see the need for; they are elated when they see the differences that have been made.

Should they have the resources, they are then inclined to want to build on the successes achieved. By repeating the cycle outlined to this point, the emerging campaign builds constituency as it creates a greater community of purpose with each passing year. This stands in stark contrast to many campaigns that have secured ever-larger amounts from fewer and fewer donors while depleting constituent depth.

Campaigns, like all human phenomena, benefit from objective review and a willingness to see a situation for what it is. The simple truth, as any veteran campaigner will tell you, is that most people who give during these times do not do so because an institution is in a campaign, but rather because the campaign has clarified its purposes and allowed them to see themselves in one of them.

These same veterans will also tell you that even the most successful campaigns are not about convincing legions of prospects to give to only what the institution wants. Instead, they often involve the institution responding to donor-generated ideas or simply receiving surprise gifts that come from estates or "over the transom." And, finally, they will tell you that many of those who made gifts in a given campaign were not even aware that the institution was in a campaign. This, then, is why it is far more authentic to celebrate the realization of purpose, and not the end of a somewhat artificial construct that we call a campaign.

- New realities, including changes in attitude, generational differences, and increased competition for a narrower segment of concentrated wealth, necessitate rethinking the standard approaches associated with the comprehensive campaign. While some of those approaches may have validity for well-established institutions with significant constituent depth, more and more institutions will need to adopt new approaches.

- The emergent comprehensive campaign will put more emphasis on impact-oriented initiatives and mission milestones that will be tested and proven in the first phase of the campaign, and then further leveraged in the next phase. This approach will seek to achieve a more comprehensive understanding of how institutional agency is to be defined, place less emphasis on dollars raised and more on deeds done, and spend less time on celebrating campaign success and more on a recalibration of purposes and progress every three to five years.

- The emergent model for a comprehensive campaign will be one of greater collaboration, shared talents, and more volunteer contribution in the shaping of content and defining of purposes, with much less effort spent on overt fundraising.

Campaign Timelines

Traditional Campaign

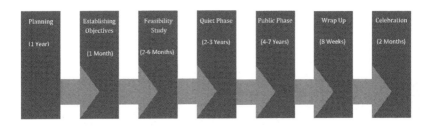

| Planning (1 Year) | Establishing Objectives (1 Month) | Feasibility Study (2-6 Months) | Quiet Phase (2-3 Years) | Public Phase (4-7 Years) | Wrap Up (8 Weeks) | Celebration (2 Months) |

Emerging Campaign

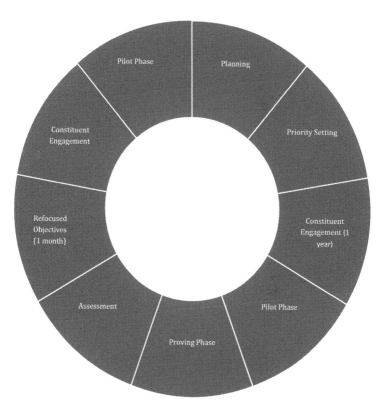

CHAPTER IX:
THE PRACTICALITIES OF CAMPAIGN PLANNING

Projecting Campaign Totals

Setting a monetary goal for the public phase of a fundraising campaign has traditionally been done after deliberating on the recommendations of a campaign consulting firm. The total is calculated employing a variety of means, including the following:

- Assessing the strength of the prospect field, including capacity (based in part on previous giving, and in part on wealth screening) and propensity (often at three levels: strong, moderate, and weak), and assuming that one gift could be secured for every three strong prospects or one for every four moderate prospects or one for every five weak prospects.

- Assessing the strength of the case, but only among a subset of the most prominent prospects (a representative sampling of the 5 percent to 10 percent of the field of prospects capable of giving 90 percent to 95 percent of the campaign total). Some campaign consulting firms have the capability of testing the opinions and attitudes of a larger sample through telephone or online surveys about specific proposed initiatives and determining which have the greatest donor appeal.

- Evaluating the size and capability of the advancement staff to secure support from the strongest prospects and to further develop the moderate and weak prospects.

The general tendency in such evaluations, however, erred on the side of finding out how much money was "out there" and sizing the campaign accordingly. It was an approach that emphasized the importance of constituent connections over the power of the case. As a result, such campaigns were far more effective in securing support from known sources than in attracting new ones. In that sense, the campaign total's projection was based on rather simplistic assumptions, extrapolations, and an underlying belief that past giving was the best predictor of future support. While valid in many ways, it understated the power of agency to attract new sources of support and to awaken latent sources, such as appreciative, but non-donating alumni.

The emerging campaign should incorporate these techniques, but create a more predictive set of models by doing the following:

- Conducting a broader and more representative assessment of constituent strengths;

- Testing the potential of particular agency-oriented initiatives to draw considerable support, including eight-figure and nine-figure lead gifts from previous donors and previously non-aligned or unaffiliated philanthropists; and

- Relying less on donor testimony shared in feasibility studies and more on donor behaviors, including giving patterns, revealed through more-extensive research.

Budgeting

The best budgeting is not done on a spreadsheet, but is an outgrowth of a larger strategic-planning exercise. Budgeting for a comprehensive campaign requires a guiding logic. For the emerging campaign, that logic goes something like this:

- Great wealth is concentrated in relatively few hands.

- The largest gifts come from those in the top 2 percent of the gift pyramid.

- A campaign cannot be successful if it does not secure large commitments from the top 2 percent.

- Institutions secure large gifts from the top 2 percent through long affiliation and/or a powerful business plan or case for support that allows the investor to understand that a gift of $10 million or $100 million will have a transformative impact. In other words, you cannot raise $100 million without a 20-year investment in relationship building or a $100-million idea and supporting plan.

- Significant effort and expense must be allocated to positioning an institution or some part of it to compete for the largest gifts possible within its prospect pools or within the reach of its greatest competencies.

- If an institution secures gifts of eight or nine figures, its fundraising expenses seem modest by comparison; if it does not, its overhead appears to be very high.

- The primary budgeting challenge is not to determine how many fundraisers an institution requires in order to pursue a population of prospects of mixed interests and propensities, but rather what it will take to achieve the following:

  o Compete for support from the top 2 percent by virtue of deepening connections and/or strengthening of campaign content. (The deepening of connection, given the stature of this subset of prospects, needs to be brokered by the president with the advancement staff, particularly the chief advancement officer and his or her senior staff; content should be generated by academic and administrative leaders with writing and editing support from advancement).

  o Launch, sustain, and prove the efficacy of the featured initiatives upon receipt of funding. (The truest form of stewardship is not the generation of thank-you notes or donor recognition, but demonstrating impact.)

  o Replicate the previous two steps for those in the top 3 percent to 10 percent of wealth in the following order: those who have given previously to the institution for 10 years or more; those who have given for five years or more; those who gave for five years or more, but ceased giving one to three years ago; alumni who have not given, but have supported initiatives similar to those spot-lighted in the campaign; and non-aligned donors whose previous philanthropic histories suggest the potential for aligning with campaign initiatives.

o Deepen the affiliation of those with the combination of strong appreciation and sig-nificant means (top 3 percent to 5 percent), but no recent affiliation to create a pipeline of short- term support for the ensuing two years.

o Replicate the step above for those whose means fall in the top 5 percent to 10 percent of wealth.

A campaign must place the greatest emphasis on agency-demonstrating initiatives for the whole to work and for an operation to generate enough revenue to reinvest in the long-term.

Most of the budget allocated to the campaign at the outset should be for the crystallization of direction and the assessment of constituent depth. When direction is crystallized into agency-demonstrating initiatives, resources must be allocated to the discovery and engagement of prospects with propensities that correspond to the institution's advertised purposes.

The pilot phase of the campaign should focus on securing the largest levels of donor investment for the initiatives that are the most implementable. Strong content-based initiatives, particularly when presented to the most significant of prospects, should be handled by presidents, board members, and academic leaders, with advancement professionals in the background conducting research, developing approach strategies, and orchestrating engagement strategies.

The emerging campaign should feature malleable and customized documents, such as white papers, and small, purpose-driven events such as salons. As noted earlier, board members should be leery of large requests for "campaign collateral materials," particularly those developed without sophisticated market research.

The second largest allocations at the outset of a campaign should be for more planning, research, and training. When those are in place, an assessment can be done to determine the right level of investment in the advancement operation, in general, and in the number of frontline fundraising professionals, in particular.

Campaign budgets can be unduly inflated when an institution does the following:

- Subscribes to the notion that every significant stakeholder (academic vice president, dean, athletic director, librarian, etc.) should have his or her own development officer or team, irrespective of their level of distinction or preparedness (lack of academic distinction, weak constituent affiliation, inability to demonstrate agency).

- Floods too few prospects with too many ideas, which confuses donors and wastes resources.

- Puts too many fundraisers in the field with weak content in pursuit of too many poorly qualified prospects.

- Gives fundraisers too many prospects to pursue, forcing them to pay inadequate attention to many at the cost of significant attention to the more promising few (75 to 90 prospects per fundraiser is about right, allowing fundraisers to spend 50 percent on the top third and, when they close, moving on to the next third, etc.).

- Fails to pay attention to the current ratio of requested meetings with prospects to the number of prospect meetings actually secured.

- Fails to monitor engagements with prospects to ensure that they are content rich.

Absent a candid assessment of appreciation, affiliation, agency and accountability, it is difficult to say what a reasonable rate of return on fundraising investment is. For mature institutions with considerable constituent depth and the ability to define and deliver on agency, the return could be 20 times the amount invested. For institutions with none of those attributes, the return could be only twice the level of investment.

Volunteers

The philanthropic return on volunteer engagement, as noted earlier, is 10 times that of the non-engaged contributor, but board members should make sure that this factor is not interpreted too simplistically and applied too carelessly. First of all, a distinction must be made between an actual volunteer—a nonpaid person who alleviates the workload of the organization and/or advances its mission in some measureable way—and a volunteer in name only who gives time, often on an advisory board, but does little beyond listening to presentations by institutional representatives and then commenting.

The use of such advisory boards has become more common based on the simplistic notion that putting someone on a board is an effective form of cultivating a major gift. Yet if those recruited for board service are wealthy, but not truly philanthropic, a parade of dog-and-pony shows will not change their essential nature. If, on the other hand, someone of real talent and an impressive record of giving is recruited to work on a real set of tasks, the substantive engagement is likely to result in higher levels of giving over time.

The best way to make the most of volunteers in a comprehensive campaign is to engage them in agency-oriented task forces and working groups. The least effective way is to place them on campaign steering committees with the hope that it will inspire them to give more than they would otherwise or to raise money, by virtue of their stature, from non-affiliated peers. Both assumptions are naïve.

The simple truth is that most volunteers do not like fundraising and are not particularly effective at it. Better volunteers will be attracted by offering them a chance to apply their skills to high-impact tasks, such as shaping institutional strategy or helping to build coalitions around specific initiatives, which, in turn, will inspire them to give larger amounts and to serve as advocates with their peers. Further, fewer and fewer highly active and accomplished leaders have time to engage in ceremonial campaign duties or attend frequent campaign meetings. If people of significance are lured into serving on committees that have flimsy agendas, their confidence in the institution will wane.

Institutions that create large campaign committees, sometimes for political purposes or out of the mistaken belief that they will be fundraising engines, discover that they are undercutting overall fundraising productivity by pulling some of their best fundraisers on staff out of the field and to spend more fruitless time cajoling campaign volunteers to fulfill their assignments. Frontline fundraising is best left to the most seasoned professionals, but well-chosen volunteers can be of immense value in brokering connections to significant prospects and helping the institution make an investment case for targeted initiatives.

The tradition of recruiting prominent alumni, parents, and other key constituents to a national or international campaign committee with subcommittees in various geographical regions is proving to be of limited value. This approach was based on the belief that impressive names on a campaign masthead would lend gravitas to the campaign, inspire the support of a broader base of donors, serve as an effective form of cultivation for those recruited, and inspire them to give more than they would otherwise. While that might have been true at one time and might still have an impact in places where there is a well- established power structure, today donors are increasingly self- directed in their philanthropic decisions and much less apt to follow the example of others or to be motivated by sitting on a campaign committee.

However, a well-constructed campaign steering committee —one that is made up of representatives of key internal and external constituencies (faculty, staff, students, alumni, parents, and others)— can be an effective way of giving those stakeholders and the groups they represent a voice in the campaign, but only if they play an active role in all phases, beginning with strategic planning. In this way, the agendas of various constituents can be forged into one, facilitating communication and community building.

However, institutional leaders should ask one important question about representational campaign committees:

How do we ensure that the representatives actually communicate to their constituencies? Various constituencies not only want to have a place at the table, they also want to know their voices are being heard, their ideas are being shared by their representatives, and that they will be kept apprised of critical decisions throughout the process.

Board members should assist their institutions in the identification and recruitment of highly talented volunteers. The best way to do this is by finding people who have done similar jobs in an exemplary way and convincing them that their talents can be applied to even more rewarding ends at your organization.

Stewardship

All too often, stewardship is thought of as simply thanking participants. Yet the definition that is most appropriate to the comprehensive campaign is that stewardship means looking after one's property. In this case, the property in question is the gifts that have been given to the institution by its donors. While most institutions adequately thank their donors, usually immediately after the gift is given, too few institutions help donors understand the impact of their gift, especially over time. There is no better way to retain donors and instill loyalty than by helping them see how their gift lives on and will live on, whether made in the form of endowment or not.

Board members can play an invaluable role in making stewardship an institutional ethic by doing the following:

- Asking to be briefed on how significant donors receive updates on their endowments and the impact of funds disbursed from them, and how other major gift donors are apprised of the ongoing or growing significance of a gift they may have made five, 10, or even 20 years ago.

- Personally calling on some of the institution's most significant contributors, including modest, but very loyal donors (15 years or more), to inquire about their satisfaction with the institution's stewardship of their gift and, by extension, to let it be known that donors' satisfaction is a matter to which the board pays close attention.

KEY TAKEAWAYS

- Projections of campaign totals should be based on a multivariate analysis, and more rigorous assessment of prospect viability that goes beyond wealth screening.

- Campaign budgeting should include both a top down approach—understanding the importance of a strong emphasis on securing principal and major gifts—and a bottom up approach, to ensure that the institution builds constituent capacity over time.

- The development and implementation of a volunteer engagement plan will improve significantly the probability of an institution securing a much larger quotient of major gifts provided that the focus is on recruiting volunteers with strong, pre-existing philanthropic propensities, and that those volunteers are afforded opportunities to apply their skills to meaningful tasks.

- The stewardship of an institution's most valuable donors should be elevated to a board level responsibility.

CHAPTER X: CONCLUDING THOUGHTS

Institutions that aspire only to secure funds for the traditional categories of support, including scholarship and fellowships, faculty support, and capital improvements need not incur the additional expense of a comprehensive campaign. Or put another way, the bells and whistles of a comprehensive campaign, including tonier events and expensive collateral material, will not help an institution raise more money for basic purposes. And no amount of expense or effort will compensate for an idea that is out-of-sync with market realities, such as a campaign simply to build endowment or to raise funds to help pay for already-built buildings.

The increase in the number of organizations seeking donations, the growth of advancement operations, and the increasingly sophisticated means of identifying and engaging sources of private support have bred far more discerning donors. These donors, with the benefit of experience in giving to multiple institutions and with the power of comparison shopping, are demanding that institutions demonstrate greater accountability and outline the potential impact of the funds raised when they ask for support. And, increasingly, they are demonstrating less willingness to support institutions and more interest in funding specialized initiatives that resonate with their values and interests.

Meanwhile, philanthropic alumni, the most likely and obvious source of support for colleges and universities, are migrating to other causes and purposes, a trend that has been masked by larger gifts to institutions from an aging and increasingly narrow segment of the population. No institution of higher learning, no matter its current strength, can afford to avoid these new realities. Those that accept that they are real and not apt to change or revert to the way things used to be can prosper in the face of change. Adaption to change is not selling out or acquiescing to donor demands; it is a matter of aligning purposes and creating enduring reciprocal relationships. Those qualities are the key to sustained support.

Even if an institution currently is not in a position to conduct a comprehensive campaign, its board members could render no greater service than by asking these questions:

- What would it take for us to be ready to mount a campaign and how long would it take?

- What can we do to strengthen the appreciation of students for their educational experience here and encourage them to want to retain ties to this institution over the long term?

- How can we strengthen the affiliation of alumni and other key constituents and do so in a way that allows us to become the beneficiaries of their talents, life experiences, and animating passions? Related to this, how can we re-conceive the workforce that constitutes an institution of higher learning so that volunteers are a more valuable and integral part of it?

- How can we sharpen our strategic focus to ensure the relevance of this institution in the decade ahead? How can we better understand how our strengths relate to larger societal needs and opportunities? Where can we best demonstrate agency, and thereby inspire the highest possible levels of private support?

Answering those questions and moving in the directions the answers suggest will build fundamental and adaptable strength for the institution. While the times may call for more discernment and reflection before launching a comprehensive campaign, particularly the traditional form, they also offer hope for any institution that commits itself to creating the conditions for success by addressing issues of appreciation, affiliation, agency and accountability. These are the building blocks of institutional greatness that will eventually set the stage for a more efficient and workable means of securing larger amounts of sustainable support through the model of the emerging comprehensive campaign.

ABOUT THE AUTHOR

JAMES M. LANGLEY

Founder and President, Langley Innovations

Before forming his own comprehensive advancement consulting firm, Jim served as vice president for advancement at Georgetown University. At Georgetown, he led the institution's offices of alumni affairs, strategic communications and marketing, development, medical center development, and advancement services. During his tenure, he produced record numbers in new commitments and dollars, despite a difficult economy. He also launched a number of innovative programs, including the acclaimed Student Discovery Initiative.

Jim arrived at Georgetown after spending eight years as the vice president for advancement at the University of California, San Diego. At UCSD, he led the planning and execution of the institution's seven- year $1 billion campaign, then raised almost half the target amount in three years, despite a weak economy. Jim also previously served as vice president for external affairs at Georgia Institute of Technology, increasing annual gift income from $26 million to $76 million and more than tripling the institution's endowment to well over $500 million. Operations under his management have won awards in virtually every area of university advancement.

Made in the USA
San Bernardino, CA
07 August 2018